D1577798

CREATIVE MEDITATION

CREATIVE MEDITATION

By

CARLETON WHITEHEAD

DODD, MEAD & COMPANY

NEW YORK

Library of Congress Cataloging in Publication Data
Whitehead, Carleton.
  Creative meditation.

  1. Spiritual life, 2. Success. I. Title.
BL624.W47   248′.4   75-4882
ISBN 0–396–07139–2

To all of the many students through the years who, with their deep desire to learn, challenged me to present spiritual and mental principles in understandable terms, this book is affectionately dedicated.

ACKNOWLEDGMENTS

To the many who have contributed guidance and encouragement in the publishing of this book, my deep appreciation, especially to:

Dr. Ernest Holmes and Dr. Harvey S. Hardman for their many years of inspiration and instruction.

Elena Goforth Whitehead for her inspired and invaluable way with words.

Joan L. Bonnett for her over-view and skill in bringing the material into finished form.

CONTENTS

PREFACE

There is one desire we all have in common. That is the desire to be in control of our own lives, to know that what we experience in living need not be a matter of "fate," luck, happenstance, or activity predestined by some unknown entity outside ourselves. How you and I *can* control our lives, shape our future, and make our tomorrow better than our today or yesterday is the subject of this book.

We live in a universe of law and order, governed by universal principles operating in exact and predictable ways. These principles, invisible and unseen, are the creation of an Intelligence beyond our human understanding, and we are now awakening to and discovering Its infinite possibilities for the enrichment of our lives.

One of the first truths this awakening and discovery reveals is that there is a deeper meaning to existence than we were previously aware of, and that we are by nature spiritual. Our bodies and the physical world of things are but avenues for the expression of something far greater.

A spiritual person is not one who spends half his wak-

ing time on his knees and the other half not doing things
he shouldn't. Nor is the person who has awakened to this
creative Intelligence, part of his Inner Self, a weakling
shrinking from life. He is strong, with confidence that
grows as he stands on his spiritual feet and uses his spiritual resources to enrich every phase of his existence. He
realizes that the spiritual realm within, the dynamic realm
of Mind, is the very center of Life. With this realization
he begins to glimpse the potential of an Inner Kingdom,
imbued with the qualities and capabilities of a higher
Intelligence and Power.

Infinite Mind, which is the one creating Intelligence, is
universal and thus centered in each person—in *you*. When
you think, It thinks—amazing as this may seem. When you
entertain an idea, the creative process responds as would
a manufacturing plant when you place an order. The
details of design are formulated, as are the plans for carrying through to the finished product.

Power, the same power that evolves a majestic oak tree
from a tiny acorn, acts through your belief. It reaches out
with the great law of attraction to draw to you all the
elements necessary to the design. Directed by Intelligence,
this action takes place harmoniously in the right sequence.

The idea you animate with your belief actually grows
into expression. Knowing this, you turn your thought and
lift your vision to the person you want to be, the circumstances and conditions you want to experience, trusting
that Universal Mind, Power, Intelligence has already begun to manifest your desired good.

The principle of the creative process is that an image

which becomes real in thought is translated into action by the Law of Mind.

You can tune in to the abundant good the universe holds for you through an orderly, concise, and proven method called *spiritual mind treatment*. This *process* is the management of an idea in thought (mind) at the highest possible level of potential for good. It is the technique for tuning one's consciousness to Mind, the unlimited and ever-present dynamic creator.

What you consistently and persistently entertain in your mind becomes your experience, and you can train your mind to entertain only that which you want to manifest in your life. Persisted in and practiced regularly, spiritual mind treatment releases the riches of your Inner Kingdom into ever greater avenues of expression, beneficial and harmonious for all concerned.

Demonstration of desired good in your life through definite and applied spiritual mind treatment proves to you the dynamic power of your mind when consciously attuned to the Universal Mind of your Inner Self, the One Source of all good. To demonstrate your cherished good is to manifest in experience that which began as a thought or an idea in your consciousness.

By applying the principles set forth in the seven steps of creative meditation which follow, you can demonstrate, as many others have done, more expansive, joyful living: health and vitality, self-fulfillment, prosperity, success, freedom from worry, better human relationships, and—above all—the peace and serenity evolving from the realization that you can and do control your own experience because you know how to manage your Dynamic Mind.

PART ONE

Learning the Seven Steps of Creative Meditation

INTRODUCTION

Creative meditation at the spiritual level involves both a tuning in and a giving out. Inflow and outflow, like receiving and giving, are complements of one action. The action is complete only when both elements are present.

The *tuning in* to Infinite Mind is a receiving of light, inspiration, and intuition, along with an awareness of creative power. Creation is the *giving out* into expression that which has been received. It is the contemplation of power, guided by light, producing the particular good desired. The ensuing outer action is carried forward into manifestation by the natural Law of Mind. This manifestation completes the creative cycle and bears witness to the truth, just as a flower bears witness to life.

A clearly defined technique or method for moving into the creative process is of great help. It provides a way of opening the consciousness to the spontaneous action of Spirit, in which the universal creative process becomes individualized.

The following seven steps comprise such a method, called creative meditation or *spiritual mind treatment,* incorporating the fundamental principles essential to complete action. The first four steps are those of inflow, or tuning in. They bring to the center of awareness the nature of Mind and Spirit, and a recognition of the inherent power to create. The last three steps are those of outflow or creation. They involve your inalienable right of choice as to how this power will express itself in your world.

In taking these seven steps you are following a normal, natural sequence of the learning process with which you are already familiar. You first become aware of and consider an idea intellectually until it is clarified in your thinking. Then as you continue giving attention to it mentally, or objectively, as being valid, it becomes a habitual part of your thinking, establishing itself subjectively. Thus you let the idea flow easily from an intellectual perception and acceptance of it toward an actual *feeling,* or emotional belief in it.

For example, during Step One in the process of creative meditation you consider intellectually that there is only one Mind, one creating Intelligence, one Power, one God. You do not need to accept this idea in a leap of "blind faith." You think about and question the reality of it until you clearly understand it objectively, intellectually. You mentally observe the reasonableness of it and that it harmonizes with that which is observed scientifically in the universe. In this way you are *moving toward a feeling acceptance* of the idea of the one Mind and of the fundamental unity of being.

The following lessons and spiritual mind treatments

will help you to think creatively, to learn the process of moving freely from the state of objective perception of your desired good to your subjective acceptance of it, the place from which your manifest experience actually arises. After studying each of the lessons, declare the spiritual mind treatment accompanying it silently or aloud, allowing your thought to dwell consciously on its meaning. This continued definite practice brings a heightened awareness of the nature of Mind and a fulfilling sense of well-being into every area of your intellect, emotion, and body.

CHAPTER 1

CLARIFY

Clarify your belief about the nature of Mind, Universal Intelligence, Spirit, God.

Think about the reality that "Mind is one," "God is one," that there is only one creating Intelligence, until the light of this truth begins to shine in your consciousness, dissolving the darkness of duality. Even clearer becomes the realization of *one* source, *one* intelligence, *one* power, universally present here and now. Contemplate the nature of this Oneness existing as the all-pervading and ever-present qualities of Life, Love, Light, Power, Peace, Beauty, and Joy. Let your awareness of these qualities come alive.

The Oneness of the Universe

Spiritual wisdom proclaims—and modern science verifies— the fundamental unity of all things. There is ONE God— ONE Creative Power, ONE Intelligence, ONE Ultimate Reality expressing in a multitude of forms. Creative Power and Intelligence constitute this forever invisible Reality, and visible forms are but Its changing expressions.

Our growing awareness of the Unity of the UNIverse

is our conscious contact with God. We are in and of this Unity. We are in God and God is in us. We are one with the Source of Intelligence and Creative Power. We direct this Greater Power with the same authority that engineers use in directing the lesser powers of electricity, steam, and dynamite. Creative Power acts through the Law of Mind. It flows into action taking the *form* of what we believe— what we really believe with complete conviction. Our experience bears this out.

Armed with this certain knowledge of Divine Authority, we believe *only* in good. We step forward with eager expectation and overflowing gratitude into the wonderful good that is ours now.

TREATMENT

I Acquaint Myself with Mind

God is the Universal Presence present where I am. God is the infinite Knower knowing me as a unique individualization of the One Mind, Life, and Action which God is also. God, the indwelling Spirit, is forever saying, "Seek me with all your heart and you will surely find me." I heed the call. To this great adventure in discovery, I open wide my heart and mind. As with a beloved friend, I nurture the growing acquaintance.

Into my receptive consciousness flows the higher wisdom. My decisions are directed to life's larger purpose. My way is clear. My path is illumined. My expanding awareness is at peace as I behold the harmonious activity of One Power moving in and through every phase, facet, and relationship of my experience.

As my active and conscious participation in the divine partnership increases, my understanding of creation deepens. To my clearing vision, the wider perspective appears. Now I see on every hand the good I sought, the good prepared for me from the foundations of the world.

*   *   *

The Power Behind Your Idea

It is natural for an idea to flow easily into expression. If this is so, why do some of our ideas fail to produce the experiences we desire? For the answer we turn to the nature of the power behind the idea and the way it acts. When the nature of this power is understood, its use moves out of the realm of guesswork into the area of intelligent cooperation, producing consistent results. This is the way of science in all its fields of endeavor.

What is the nature of this power that uses an idea as an instrument of its action as, say, the power of electricity uses a toaster or a light bulb? Consider the axiom of applied science: "The nature of the instrument must correspond to the nature of the power." The nature of an instrument of electrical power is electrical; of mechanical power, mechanical; of chemical power, chemical. Know the nature of one and you know the nature of the other.

The essential nature of an idea is thought. Therefore the nature of the power that acts through it must be thought. And, because it has the capacity to animate the idea (coordinate all its various aspects and forge them into a new experience), it must be living, intelligent, creative thought. Furthermore, since it can act simultaneously on everyone's ideas, it must be universal. The only conceivable power of this nature is Mind. How wonderful to know that Infinite Wisdom has provided such a magnificent power for our constructive use!

Belief is like the volume knob on your radio: It controls the flow of power. The greater your belief, the greater the flow of Mind Power into your chosen idea. Your belief is strengthened through realizing that the universal, living, intelligent, creative power of Mind is always seeking your ideas as instruments of its action. More power flows, more consistent results appear—which again strengthen your belief. Thus do you become increasingly effective as the instrument for good that God intended you to be.

TREATMENT

The Presence of God Is the Power of My Life

The Presence of God around and within me is the source of my being, the light of my life, and the power of my consciousness. There is no other source, light, or power. All my experiences form as light and power flow from the one source through my beliefs and anticipations.

As a spiritual being, I know my birthright to be the freedom to choose what I will believe and anticipate. Thus no one else can interfere with my good. I fear none. No condition or circumstance can bind me. The very way in which light and power flow through me is my salvation, for I alone select my thoughts.

I wholeheartedly accept full responsibility for what I think, choose, decide, believe, and anticipate. I think of the healthy, the harmonious, and the abundant. I choose the way that produces good for all. I decide on right action. I believe in my goals. God prospers and blesses me as light and power flow through the exhilarating, fulfilling activities I anticipate bringing to pass.

*   *   *

The Reality of "Super" Natural Miracles

What an exciting age this is! It started with a battle between science and religion and is now seeing these two approaches to life coming ever closer together. Hardly a day passes without a report in a newspaper, magazine, or scientific journal of the discovery of another heretofore missing link in the chain of events connecting invisible causes with visible effects. The frontiers of the "supernatural" are being steadily pushed back as the spirit of truth rides the vanguard of both science and religion.

We are learning that this great universe of ours is mental and spiritual as well as physical, and that all three realms are governed by laws through which the One Creative Power flows into manifold expression. It is our growing awareness of the reliability and *naturalness* of these laws that enables us to rise to new levels of achievement.

Miracles have long been thought of as supernatural. In

one sense this is true; in another it is not. One definition of "supernatural" is "beyond the natural"; that is, by divine intervention, a temporary setting aside of a law or laws of the universe. This position presumes an arbitrary authority in the cosmos, a premise that is untenable to the scientific mind. Another definition is "supremely natural," a result or results obtained through complete coordination with all the natural laws involved.

An illustration of the latter is the "miraculous" return of spaceship Apollo 13. From the moment trouble developed, all minds in the Odyssey and at the Space Center were focused on the natural laws of gravity, power, action and reaction with a single thought: "How can these laws be coordinated into one successful action?" On the answer hung the lives of three men. The precise use of the above laws, with timing to a fraction of a second, was accomplished at four critical points along the course. The result landed the spacecraft safely on an incredibly small target. Thought and decision perfectly coordinated with law produced the "supremely natural" miracle. An accompanying miracle was taken for granted. People around the world watched the splashdown *as it happened.* This "natural" witnessing of events was possible because men combined their thoughts and aspirations with the nature of electronics.

These examples plus a thousand you can add, from A-irplanes to Z-oom lenses, make a strong case for stating that miracles result not from *inter*vention but from *in*-vention. Invention means "the coming into" or discovery of natural relationships that produce what was previously considered impossible.

Now, since natural laws and relationships are created by Mind, all "miracle-producing" combinations are known in Mind, awaiting discovery. When consciousness is tuned to Mind by spiritual attentiveness and singleness of purpose (as with Apollo 13), it makes this discovery and becomes the instrument of "supernatural" action. In this light, most of our experiences are unnatural and subnormal, while miracles are both natural and normal. They are gifts of God seeeking you to happen through. Expect them!

TREATMENT

I Tune My Consciousness to God

God is where I am. The One Presence surrounds me. The divine qualities of Life, Love, and Light encompass me. This is not a blind affirmation; it is a statement of truth, for separation from the Infinite is impossible.

I am not deluded by belief in any power other than Good. Negatives are less than nothing, and I waste no thought and emotion on minus quantities. Only the positive, the good, the whole, and the harmonious are worthy of my attention.

Using my inalienable right of choice, I tune my consciousness to Reality. With marvelous response, the cells of my body vibrate with Life. They unite in actions that flow in the pattern of wholeness. Every string of my emotional being throbs with overtones of the fundamental

Love. The harmony in my heart hears its echo in all my relationships. Light radiates in my mind, and my illuminated awareness perceives creation's order and beauty. Attunement has set me on the path that leads from glory to glory.

*   *   *

To perceive intellectually and then to *feel* the truth of the oneness and fundamental unity of all expression is the first step of creative meditation. This realization is your point of contact with the Power of Mind. Once this is clarified in consciousness, you are ready to take the next step, that of identifying *your* mind, yourself, with Infinite Mind.

CHAPTER 2

IDENTIFY

Identify yourself with Mind, God; where you are,
God is.

Identify yourself with God. As the Infinite Spirit, Mind, and Life, God is everywhere present and is therefore present in you as the reality of your being. Meditate on statements of truth such as: "Where I am, God is. I am an individualization of the spirit of God. My mind is one with the Mind of God. I am alive with the life of God. God in me, as me, is me."

Recognition of your true identity usually begins with your intellectual acceptance of it. Then, continued thinking on the reality of your being opens awareness at ever-deeper levels of consciousness. With this grows the realization that "I am one with God, and the qualities of Life, Love, Light, Peace, Power, Beauty, Joy in me, of me, are forever seeking fuller expression through me."

Your Real Identity

Silently, softly the snow is falling, tiny individual flakes floating down, millions upon millions of them. Yet each one is unique. There are no two alike. Each is an artistic gem. All are of the same substance. Yet each has its own identity.

Like these beautiful crystals are people. All are of the one Spirit, the one Mind, and the one Substance. Yet the body bears witness to the fact that each person is unique. Every organ, every cell—not just fingertips—bears the stamp of this uniqueness. What is this physical evidence saying to us? What else but: "You are specially designed by the Infinite Artist. You have a definite identity in the Spirit and Mind of God. You have something to give, do, and be that is separate and distinct, something that no other can give, do, or be."

The identity of a snowflake remains intact as it floats down with others in response to the forces of air and gravity. This identity is not in form only but in action also. Each flake, due to its shape and size, responds individually to the forces around it. It is not governed by what other flakes do, how many or how few there are. It is purely itself. Only when the action ceases and one flake piles upon another is the identity lost.

You express your Divine uniqueness when your responses to the forces of life arise from your inner identity rather than from the multitudes of public opinions and pressures. What you are—to give, do, and be—is stifled if you "let the world around you squeeze you into its own mold," as Paul put it (Romans 12:2, Phillips translation).

Unlike the snowflake, which must at last become part of the mass, you have the right and power of choice. Fear cannot force you into conformity with the crowd. Even if you should succumb to the forces of conformity, your true identity, again unlike the snowflake, is inviolate. You can choose to "let God remold your mind from within" (Romans 12:2). You can choose to reactivate your Divine identity . . . the artistic gem which you are.

TREATMENT

God Expresses as Me

God is the Spirit, Mind, and Essence of Life universally present. Therefore, right where I am, God is. My spirit is the Spirit of God. My mind is the Mind of God. My being is the very Essence of the One, uniquely individualized as me.

The light of this fundamental truth radiates into every area of my thought and feeling. All dark and hidden fears are dissipated, leaving me free to move in all relationships with faith and trust. Dissolved are all shadowy doubts of my capacity to meet the challenges of growth. I face each one with the certain awareness that the Spirit which I am knows only victory.

My body, formed of the One Life Essence, is charged with universal energy. Designed in wholeness and health, it is the truly wonderful instrument of the Spirit and Mind of God which I am.

From my mind flows a continuous stream of ideas that pours life, love, and inspiration into every situation I encounter. Action is revitalized, harmonized, and lifted into a new dimension of creativity. I glory in the expression of God as me.

*   *   *

The Winning Combination

In sports a coach is always seeking the winning combination of talent, teamwork, and confidence. Against such a combination the opponents are outmaneuvered and outplayed. This is also true in the game of life. However, in sports, where there is a winner there is also a loser. In the game of life everyone can be a winner.

In sports the opponents are obvious. In life they are more subtle. Paul wrote, "We wrestle not against flesh and blood . . ."; we wrestle against defeatist attitudes, fears, and false ideas. Opponents are within, not without, and the team that can sweep them off the field is sitting right on your bench. Here is the roster: Truth, Talent, Faith.

Truth. The Truth is that you are a creation of Infinite Mind, a Divine idea designed to fulfill life, to succeed, to be a winner. False ideas of inadequacy, inferiority, and their cronies do not stand a chance against this star!

Talent. As a Divine idea in Mind you are equipped with everything necessary for victory. You are one with the Source of power, wisdom, and love. Fears of insecurity, failure, and rejection fade before this array of talent!

Faith. As the truth that you are an individualization of Divine Mind sparks your inexhaustible talents, *faith* comes onto the field. It is the faith of God in you filling your entire consciousness. Defeatist attitudes shrivel before it!

This is your "team" for the game of life. You are the coach and captain. You choose the goals. You call the plays. Knowing this, you practice with the members until perfect teamwork is established. Growing awareness of the truth that you are God-created and sustained sparks your talents. Power for good flows through you into every area of your life. Wisdom guides your decisions and inspires great ideas. Love radiates from the core of your being, dissolving all opposition. Faith is your natural attitude, permeating every thought. It imbues every act with poise and confidence.

Through devotion, persistence, and acceptance of your responsibility as coach and captain you have blended your team into the winning combination. Victory in the game of life is yours!

TREATMENT

God Is My Partner

God is not a far-off being but a warm, living Presence within me and around me. I am becoming more vitally aware of this Presence. I know that God is at all times my friend, my Silent Partner in my every endeavor, my every hope, my every ambition. This Inner One is always ready with Divine Intelligence to mold the right idea at the right time in exactly the right way. Instantly available to this Partnership is the Creative Power necessary to vitalize the idea and bring it forth into manifestation.

I love and trust my Silent Partner. I rely completely upon this wisdom and guidance to lift my desire into the realm of All Good. I have implicit faith in Its Creative Power bringing forth my desire into my experience. In the high consciousness of this Divine Partnership, I speak the word of my desire, and I *know* the result is inevitable. And so it is.

*   *   *

Your Most Priceless Possession

That God is not a copy artist is demonstrated by the fact that each grain of sand, leaf, snowflake, and fingerprint is distinct among billions of relatives. This perpetual inventiveness, while fascinating and awe-inspiring at the physical level, is of profound significance at the spiritual level, for it reveals your most priceless possession: your God-created uniqueness. You are a spiritual idea designed to express a special facet of the Infinite, to give to the world what no one else can.

When we neither understand nor appreciate our originality, we fabricate masks that we hope will please others, an impossible goal. The result is conflict and frustration, with their consequent sickness and sorrow.

Sage advice for uncovering your treasure comes from William James: "Seek out that particular mental and moral attitude which makes you feel most deeply and vitally alive, along with which comes the inner voice which says 'this is the real me,' and when you have found that attitude, follow it."

TREATMENT

Today I Am Born Anew

The only begotten son of God is the potential of perfection at the center of man—the indwelling Divinity. Con-

powerful

ceived in Wisdom, born in Love, the Divine Image is the
eternal promise of the kingdom, the power, and the glory.
It is the way, the truth, and the life. It is what God is in
me as my Self.

Misconceptions never alter reality. Even though I may
have entertained every false and limited belief thought by
man, my true nature is unchanged. Knowing this, I open
my mind and my heart to the God-created idea of me.
Light radiates into every area of my consciousness. The
shadows of error are no more. Love permeates my thought
and emotion, dissolving all unlike itself. The Law of
Harmony governs my life. Truth sets me free.

Born, growing, and waxing strong is the *conscious*
awareness of my Divine Self. Warm, loving, and vital are
the thoughts of joy, peace, and goodwill that flow from me
with increasing power to all people—everywhere.

*   *   *

The Image

The remarkably lifelike little wooden bear at Yellowstone
Park Trading Post caught my eye. I asked the man who
carved it how he achieved such realism. He smiled. "It is
very simple," he said. "I choose a block of wood the desired size and look at it until I see the bear inside. Then
I cut away the excess wood."

How similar to this is the emergence of the Divine Self
from the block of human personality! The God-created
image within is revealed and the unique individualization
of the Divine which you are comes forth not by accumulat-

ing qualities, characteristics, and powers you do not possess, but by eliminating thoughts, traits, and reactions foreign to your true nature. Life, love, wisdom, and power are inherent. Their opposites are but accretions to be cut away.

As you contemplate yourself, seeking to see the Divine Image within, the outline may seem very dim. But as you continue to cut away the excess, the eternal God-created image in you, as you, appears.

TREATMENT

Where I Am, God Is

God is the infinite reality. That which is infinite is everywhere present; therefore, right where I am, God is. Where God is, there is life, intelligence, and creative power.

The Life that is living itself in me is the Life of God. This is the Life eternal and therefore ageless. It is as fresh and as new as this moment in which I contemplate it. I am not an accumulation of years; I am a beloved individualization of Mind that brought me into being. Life, flowing in me under the direction of Mind, maintains my body as the healthy instrument of God-consciousness, which it is.

As God-consciousness, I am the outlet of new, unique, and prosperous ideas flowing from Mind and seeking expression by means of me. This creative action is producing beauty, harmony, and joy in my experience and in the experience of those with whom I come in contact. I rejoice

in knowing that the world is being constantly improved
because I know that where I am, God is.

*   *   *

With your true identity and nature established in your
thinking, you are ready to widen your horizons and move
forward in your creative thinking. Your growing understanding and acceptance of your real identity—your divine
nature—open the way for further perception of the divinity, fundamental harmony, and unity that exist in *all*
creation.

CHAPTER 3

UNIFY

Unify all of creation in your consciousness with the
simple recognition of the fundamental unity of being:
In the Infinite Mind, all are one.

Unify all of creation in your consciousness with the simple recognition of the fundamental unity of being. God is one and God is all. Say to yourself, "In the Infinite Spirit, Mind, and Being, I am one with all people." As this sense of unity expands in consciousness, the truth of it glows and illuminates a profound realization: *Any action that truly benefits one, benefits all.* A living awareness of this dissolves both fear and resentment. Furthermore, it establishes in your consciousness the Law of Harmony. This law now guides you in all of your choices and decisions in a way that insures good and prosperous action for you and all concerned.

The Law of Harmony

Five men inch their way up an icy, precipitous mountain slope, bound together by a rope. Well they understand the Law of Harmony. Right action for one is right action for all. Right action for the group is right action for each individual. Even as the mists engulf them and their movements are hidden from one another, there is no temptation toward isolated action. Rather, attention to right action intensifies, with each one knowing that not only their goal, but their lives, depend upon complete devotion to the Law of Harmony. An overall idea encompasses and directs each one.

In the climb we are making toward our goal of healthier, happier, more effective living, the ties that link us to our fellow climbers, though invisible, are no less real. Because these ties are invisible, what constitutes "right action" may be difficult to determine. Yet it must be sought, because there is a spiritual Law of Harmony which demands that, in any activity, what is good for one must be good for all concerned, and what is good for all concerned must be good for the good of each one involved. Why? Because we live in a spiritual system, with unity its principle, one mind its action. The rapidly accumulating evidence of science, on all levels, bears increasing witness to this fact. Gain at another's expense is not immoral; it is impossible, regardless of superficial observation to the contrary.

The problem is how to treat for some specific activity involving others and unquestionably mesh with the Law of Harmony, for human vision can rarely foresee the full consequences. The problem is solved in two steps: (1) Realize that in Divine Mind there is always a larger idea of good that can include all concerned as well as encompass and direct the unfoldment of your desired activity; (2) let your attention and desire be completely devoted to the guidance toward right action issuing from the intelligence of the larger idea.

As your good manifests, you sense the accomplishment and exhilaration of our climbers atop the mountain, viewing grandeur far beyond their anticipation.

TREATMENT

I Am Prospered by the Harmony of Life

God is one, in all and through all. This Truth of truths fills my consciousness. The unity of being is alive in my awareness. The fundamental harmony of the Infinite Spirit permeates my thought and feeling. I sense the kinship I share with all life and with each unique manifestation of life.

I am clear in the principle that my good is inseparable from the good of the whole. Any and all fallacious belief that I could gain at another person's expense, or that another person could gain at mine, is permanently dissolved in the full recognition that my supply of life, love, abundance, and joy flows directly from the one inexhaustible Source, which is equally available to everyone.

I am constantly tuned to the universal harmony flowing beneath all appearance of discord. In this attunement I see misunderstandings clear. I witness diverging views and discover their common aim. I find the energy of conflict channeled into unified purpose. I rejoice as miracles manifest through my realization of God in and through all.

*   *   *

Dynamic Balance

Deep within everyone is the desire for peace. Turmoil in one's experience intensifies this desire, and human thinking often equates peace with cessation of activity. This would be death. Actually the desire is for vital peace, or *dynamic balance*—the smooth, harmonious, effortless movement toward the accomplishment of our purposes in all areas of life.

In the power plant 600 feet below the crest of Hoover Dam is an example of dynamic balance and a lesson on how to attain it. Here are seventeen huge generators busily converting waterpower into electrical power, supplying the needs of millions of people. Each generator, eighteen feet in diameter and weighing tons, rests on a twenty-four-inch vertical steel shaft. Below the generator on the shaft is the turbine, which is spun by thousands of gallons of water per second, striking it with a thrust of 36,000 pounds per square foot. Yet with all of this thundering force spinning tons of steel, there is not the slightest vibration—only the vital throb of tremendous power flowing smoothly, harmoniously, effortlessly, under perfect control, to fulfill its purpose. The dynamic balance is accomplished by a uniform distribution of weight, force, and action centered on the supporting shaft.

A primary principle emphasized in creative meditation is that the *only* support for the life of the individual is Divine Mind. To the degree, then, that the consciousness of the individual is centered on this support, with *all* his thought, feeling, and action radiating from it, is he dynamically balanced and moving smoothly, harmoniously, and effortlessly toward the accomplishment of his purposes in every area. This clarifies both the only cause and the only cure for every discord, disease, and disturbance in body, emotion, or affairs. The person's thinking about some difficulty is eccentric (ex-centric); it must then be drawn to the center and held there by a definite, conscious realization of God as this center of support—from which the One Power then flows into the area of concern establishing dynamic balance.

"Thou wilt keep him in perfect peace, whose mind is stayed on thee . . ." (Isaiah 26:3).

TREATMENT

God Indwells Everyone

God is the one life, mind, power, and spirit encompassing and infusing all creation. At any and every point where my thought rests, God is. The nature of the Divine, as beauty, order, and harmony throughout the universe, draws and holds my attention. The Light that lighteth every man beckons to my recognition. I behold this Light in each one I meet, in person or in thought.

Never again will my thinking be trapped by human evaluation of race, color, creed, or nationality. My judgments are based not on physical appearance but on truth. The Spirit of God in man beckons to my recognition. I behold this sublime fact, and it forever frees me from prejudice. The poison of propaganda is permanently excluded from my consciousness.

As a son of God, I walk in love among my brothers. I rejoice as I recognize in each the wonderful, unique, and divinely different expression of the One Creating Spirit. I give thanks for my growing awareness of God indwelling everyone.

* * *

Overcoming Friction

Overcoming friction consumes more than half of your car's gasoline energy. No forward motion is produced by this— only deterioration. Since the principle involved in producing friction on the material level acts similarly on the mental level, an intelligent person asks himself: "How much energy am I wasting in my various contacts with people—energy that produces no constructive action, only wear and tear? And what can I do about it?"

The solution to any problem is always contained in the principle that underlies it. Such is the case with friction, and since it is easier to grasp the application at the material level, we begin there. Friction is the product of the force pressing two surfaces together multiplied by the coefficient of friction, or "roughness factor." Note two points. One, if the coefficient of friction is zero, no amount of pressure can cause friction (10 or $10,000 \times 0 = 0$). A 200-pound man slides on ice as readily as a 40-pound child. Two, the smoother one surface is, regardless of the other, the smaller the coefficient of friction. Therefore if one surface can be made perfectly smooth, friction is eliminated.

Common examples illustrate this principle on the mental level. Two men are held together by force of circumstances in an office. One tries to argue, the other refuses to argue; hence, no argument and no friction or wear, at least for the one who remained calm. An irate customer's anger is turned aside by a friendly smile. A hostile remark is nullified by a quiet answer. The idea of "resist not evil" works *if* it is an *inner attitude*. This brings us to an all-important third point in the parallel.

The quality of material is the major factor in the maintenance of a smooth surface (*e.g.*, precious jewels used for bearings in fine watches). On the mental level, the quality of consciousness is the major factor. A calm exterior can be created by an act of will, but it can only be maintained by a calm interior stabilized by a sense of unity with God and, therefore, mankind.

Consistent treatment reduces your "coefficient of friction" and releases energy for constructive action.

TREATMENT

Unity Perfects My Experience Today

God created this day for my benefit, filled it with unlimited potential and presented it to me at dawn. In each moment is the opportunity to become more aware of the true Self that I am, to behold the glory of creation that surrounds me, and to recognize the presence of God in all whom I meet. Every instant invites me to use the power of creative thought to bring forth the good inherent in whatever situation confronts me. Truly this is the day to seek and find the treasures of Life.

I open my mind and heart to receive the Divine gift of this day. I step out in confidence, love, and joy, knowing that these qualities flow from the wellspring of Spirit within me. I appreciate the expressions of the One Mind everywhere I look. The words I speak to another befit my recognition of this person as an individualization of God. My thought instantly penetrates to and reveals the good in every situation I encounter.

I rejoice in releasing the potential with which God has filled this day.

* * *

In the Infinite Mind, all are one—existing, moving, *being* in perfect harmony; yet, at the same time, each is expressing individually and uniquely. As the realization of this truth permeates your thinking, you can advance to the next step in your understanding of the marvelous way creative power flows from choice and decision into experience.

CHAPTER 4

SIMPLIFY

Simplify your understanding of the Law of Mind; whatever becomes a real, living belief in your consciousness flows into your experience.

Simplify your understanding of the Law of Mind, which is the way creative intelligence works. Teachers such as Jesus referred to it as a Law of Belief. Whatever takes root and becomes a living belief or reality in consciousness flows into experience. Mind supplies the intelligence, power, and substance for the entire process.

Meditate on this same process in nature. Select a seed. Let your thought enter into it and behold the living reality of the mature plant. Now follow in your imagination the movement from the first stirrings of germination through growth to the full outer form. Marvel at the way Mind performs. Recognize it as the same action that carries to fruition the mental seeds that you create. *How* the action takes place at either level is unknown. Let it be. Speculation on how a desired good can come tends to sow seeds of doubt. "Commit thy way unto the Lord [Law] . . . and he shall bring it to pass" (Psalm 37:5).

The Law of Mind

Successful application of the principles of creative meditation requires clear understanding of the term "law." Confusion arises because the term has two usages: authoritarian law and natural law.

Authoritarian law is defined as "rule or rules of conduct laid down by some authority—government, society, church, etc." The essential quality here is restriction—of the individual for the benefit of society, or society for the protection of the individual.

Natural law, as used by science, defines the *way power acts*. The "law" of electricity is the way the power of electricity acts. The essential quality of this, and every other natural law, is action. This action is limited only by man's limited understanding of it. There is no restrictive element. Rather, there is the element of expansion borne out by the expanding use of electricity corresponding to man's increasing knowledge of its law.

The Law of Mind is a natural law; it is the way *Mind power acts*. A close analogy of this action is seen in a lawn sprinkler. Connect the hose to the faucet, turn it on, and water sprays in a pattern determined by the nature and pattern of the holes in the sprinkler. If a different pattern is desired, a different sprinkler is used. But the action of the power of pressure forcing the water through hose and sprinkler remains the same.

You are connected to the Source of life. This is self-evident from the fact that you are alive. Mind power is continually pushing the substance of life through you into expression. The pattern this takes as experience is not determined by the Source any more than the spray pattern is determined by the city water supply. It is determined by the pattern and nature of your thoughts and feelings, conscious and subconscious.

This is the Law. This is the way Mind Power acts through you and for you. Changes in the nature and pattern of your consciousness naturally produce corresponding changes in your experience.

The consistent use of treatment, as exemplified in this book, changes consciousness.

"Blessed is the man . . . whose delight is in the law of the Lord" (Psalm 1).

The entire realm of science testifies that "the fear of the Lord [more accurately translated 'respect for the Law'] is the beginning of wisdom" (Psalm 111:10). Respect for the undeviating, impersonal law of electricity opened the door to intelligent use of this great power. This holds true for every natural law, including the law of Mind. Ask yourself: "Do I respect the undeviating, impersonal way in which the power of Mind acts as much as I respect the consistent action of gravity?" Clear understanding of law will always produce respect. Illustrations aid in this perception.

Consider the light in a movie projector. This pure white light passes through the film and emerges on the screen as people, places, and things, as comedy, tragedy, or travelogue, in black and white or color. Not liking what we see, we do not tamper with the screen or the light; we change the film or turn off the projector. Universal Mind is the light. Its law is the projector, continually shining the light through the film of our consciousness and onto the screen of our experience.

Prior to our knowledge of Mind we may say, "My world is made up of people, circumstances, and conditions. I will change what I do not like." We may even succeed in effecting some temporary changes. But as old patterns of experience continue to repeat, the conclusion is finally reached that outer manipulation is futile. We may even plead with the light to change, only to find that in it there is "neither variableness nor shadow of turning." All that is left to change is consciousness. As we devote our effort here, we soon discover a corresponding change in experience.

We view the action of law and our respect for it grows, as, consequently, does our wisdom. Wisely we let the spirit of truth free the consciousness of false and distorted ideas, and the spirit of love dissolve destructive emotions. The screen of experience becomes filled with beauty, respect changes to reverence, reverence to love. We know with the wise men of old, "Great peace have they which love Thy law: and nothing shall offend them" (Psalm 119:165).

TREATMENT

Mind Is the Master Builder

Mind is the master builder of my experience. Faithfully, unhurriedly, accurately it molds the outer forms of the ideas I accept. It structures conditions into which the forms fit harmoniously. Cooperating colleagues are drawn into the unfolding action. Effortlessly, wisely, effectively Mind moves to complete the house of experience. There are no strikes, shortages, or delays. I choose. Mind builds.

I honor this marvelous action of Mind by accepting only ideas worthy of me. My imaging power is focused on conceptions that enrich my life and benefit my associates. I embrace ideals that add to my spiritual stature. My attention is keyed to thoughts that enhance my health.

The infinite receptivity of Mind responds to the theme of my thought. The intelligence of Mind forms corresponding patterns. The constructing power of Mind forges the patterns into healthy, creative relationships, new dimensions of inspiration, and free-flowing channels of good. I experience life at ever higher, richer levels as I wisely, lovingly cooperate with Mind, the master builder.

*   *   *

The Law of Inertia

A primary law of physics is this: *A body remains at rest or in uniform motion in a straight line until a force is applied to it.* Inertia is the quality in matter that resists change. Your car remains at rest until power is applied as force to the rear wheels. It moves in a straight line until you apply steering force to the front wheels. It moves until the force of friction brings it to rest. In each case the rapidity of change is directly proportional to the amount of force applied and the consistency of its application.

This law applies also to the body of your affairs. There is a quality of inertia that tends to perpetuate your experiences. They will remain static or moving much as they are until a force is applied sufficient to change them. This is true because the body of your affairs reflects the body of your consciousness, and the inertia of consciousness is clearly perceived in the resistance to change of thought patterns and conditioned reflexes; *i.e.*, habits, constructive or destructive. As the physicist must reckon with the inherent, impersonal quality of inertia on the physical level, so must the metaphysicist reckon with it on the mental level.

A desired change of state or direction in experience requires first a corresponding change in consciousness. Inertia of consciousness requires a force to produce that change. The only applicable force is thought—applied Mind Power. As with your car, force is applied in the direction of the desired change. The rapidity of change is directly proportional to the force and consistency of application.

Take a treatment in this book, on prosperity for example. Read over lightly, it has little effect on the inertia of a poverty consciousness. But disciplined dwelling on its truth will exert the force necessary to change entrenched thought patterns and, by the Law of Mind, experience changes correspondingly. With your consciousness positively oriented, the law of inertia works *for* you. Your thought patterns of prosperity persist regardless of negative talk around you.

TREATMENT

I Rejoice in My Divine Authority

The power of God flowing through, and taking the form of my consciousness, authors my world of experience.

Knowing this, I affirm that I am responsible for my thinking, and consequently for my actions. I recognize that all of my behavior that is ineffective and self-defeating is the result of irrational thinking based on prejudices and false beliefs. I waste no time blaming the people and environment from which I drew these prejudices and false beliefs. Instead, I ferret these out and eliminate them from my consciousness.

I now establish all my thinking on the sound, rational basis of the presence of God around and within me along with the Law of Mind by which the power of God acts through me. I authorize only those thoughts that are in harmony with life and productive of good. I accept with thanksgiving the harmonious action of good that follows with ease and order. I rejoice in my responsibility, and with wisdom I exercise authority in my world.

*   *   *

The Law of Attraction

The forces of nature are invisible. What we observe is phenomena produced by these forces. A graphic illustration is seen in this simple experiment: Iron filings are scattered at random on a piece of glass. As a magnet is placed under the glass, the filings shift into a pattern outlining the invisible magnetic field surrounding the magnet. The individual is likewise surrounded by an invisible, mental magnetic field that is outlined by the surrounding people, conditions, and things. This is a very real force, a function of the power of Mind, and acts by a Law of Mind just as the force of the magnet acts by a Law of Magnetism.

The force of a magnet may be used in many ways—as a compass, a door latch, to lift steel bars, generate electricty, operate an electric watch, or find a needle in a haystack. The specialized use depends upon the thought of the user and his knowledge of the law involved. So it is with the magnetic force of Mind. It may be used to attract friends, favorable circumstances for a business venture, opportunities for growth, harmonious environment; in general, to attract the desirable and repel the undesirable. The specialized use depends upon the thought of the user and his knowledge of the law involved, the Law of Attraction. This law is thus defined: "Thought attracts what is like itself and repels what is unlike" (Ernest Holmes).

A major difference between the physical magnet and the mental magnet (thought) is this: A physical magnet, limited by its nature, can attract only a few types of metals, whereas man determines the nature of the mental magnet and, by observing the law that like attracts like, designs the mental magnet to attract whatever he desires. Another difference is this: Force diminishes with distance from the physical magnet, while at the mental level the force is unaffected by distance, illustrated by the case of a man drawn from halfway around the world to fill a key position.

The wise man, understanding the Law of Attraction, fills his consciousness with qualitative thoughts of what he desires to the exclusion of their opposites.

My House Is a House of Prayer

I live in the house of consciousness, the home of my thoughts and feelings and, therefore, my experiences. Here I contemplate what goes on around me. Here my emotional responses dwell. In this center new ideas are conceived and born, to be clothed by Mind with the raiment of circumstance.

As I am the only thinker in my mind, I am the host in my house of consciousness. I choose with care the guests I entertain at my table and fireside. Ideas that do not reflect wisdom, faith, and integrity are unwelcome. The door is closed to feelings that do not lighten, brighten, and warm the atmosphere. I ignore the knocks of the negatives. The voices of gloom go unanswered.

God's ideas I ask in with eager anticipation of communion. Welcomed across the threshold are these vital, harmonious, loving thoughts that are always seeking my company. My house is a house of prayer, for it is filled with the consciousness of divine perfection, and my world declares the glory of God.

*   *   *

You recognize that through the Law of Mind your experience reflects whatever beliefs have taken root in your consciousness. Thus, as of now, you invite and entertain only those thoughts you want to express as realities in your life. Your consciousness is clear and the Light is shining in it. You can now proceed to select and specify the good that you desire to manifest—and that, as an individualization of the One Mind, you deserve! Plant the seeds of your desired good that will bear witness to the truth you have perceived.

CHAPTER 5

SPECIFY

Specify the particular good you desire.

Specify the particular good you desire—the solution of a problem, the clearing of a troubled situation, prosperity, or whatever. Remember, the master teacher said, "Whatsoever things you desire when you pray, believe that you have received them and you shall have them" (Mark 11:24, R.V.). Know the *qualities* you want expressed, such as Life, Love, Light, Power, Peace, Beauty, or Joy.

Some Eastern philosophies teach that desire should be killed. In the practice of creative meditation, we believe that desire, essentially, is the impulse of life urging the individual toward a greater expression of good. Desire, then, is a prerequisite to achievement and thus to our effective use of the God-created power of Mind.

However, a major block can form if you question the spirituality of your desire. The block forms thus: (1) A vague understanding of what is spiritual effectively prevents your placing your desire in this category; (2) if you cannot place your desire in a spiritual category, you decide that it is unspiritual; (3) you feel guilty trying to use God-power for something unspiritual, and a sense of guilt degrades your desire and chokes the expression of good.

The block is removed by a clear conception of what is spiritual. Since God is life, love, beauty, good, abundance, freedom, and joy, those experiences that are in harmony with any or all of these qualities are spiritual. Those experiences that are inharmonious with any of these qualities are unspiritual. Thus material things are neither spiritual nor unspiritual because they act only the way you make them act, and the way you make them act ordains your experience in regard to them. Money of itself, for example, cannot harm anyone, and you should have plenty of it— and to spare. It is poverty, lack, limitation, sickness, and discord that are unspiritual.

The spiritually conscious individual is the one who is applying spiritual power through spiritual ideas at the point in life where he is, and at the level of his own (not someone else's) understanding. Knowing this, and knowing that you are inherently spiritual because you are an individualization of God, you use the power of Mind to bring into your experience anything and everything that will increase your awareness of life, love, beauty, good, abundance, freedom, and joy. Thus neither your desire nor its fulfillment can be unspiritual, because they combine to increase your awareness of God.

Your Picture of Tomorrow

A painter envisions a picture. He knows that the composition in his consciousness will determine the quality and outline of the finished product. With utmost care he mentally paints in what he wants and paints out what he does not want. Colors are selected that will convey the desired feeling. All this is done before a brush touches the blank canvas. All that follows emanates from this inner image.

Tomorrow (and each tomorrow of the year) is a blank canvas. On it you will paint, by word and action, a picture that will correspond to what you consciously and unconsciously envision. You are creating tomorrow today, but you have the privilege of changing any color or detail before the word is spoken or the action taken.

What is your picture of tomorrow? What do you consciously and unconsciously expect to happen? Does it correspond to the desires of your heart? Before the brush touches the canvas, paint out what does not; paint in what does, using lavishly the colors of harmony, beauty, and joy.

TREATMENT

I Rejoice in the Creations of My Consciousness

Mind is forever creating anew. The Formless is eternally taking form. Unconditioned Life is continually becoming conditioned. Mind, moving as my thoughts, creates my experience. The Formless takes the form of my ideas. Life flowing through my whole being is conditioned by qualities in my consciousness. This creative forming, conditioning action is neither past nor future; it is always *now*.

This means that my future is wide open, unfashioned, unfettered, untrammeled. My tomorrows are blank canvases, and I hold the Creator's brush. I decline to sketch images other than of the rich experiences I desire. I refuse all forms that are less than the *best* I know. Firmly rejected are all qualities opposed to the glory of living.

My future begins now. My thoughts are loving, healthy, and prosperous. The ideas I envision are constructive, expansive, beneficial to all. And they outline the highest good I can imagine. My consciousness is filled with qualities of cooperation, beauty, wholeness, harmony, and joy. With enthusiasm I live the life that Mind is creating through me.

*   *   *

Definite Ideas

The amazing developments in the use of electrical power provide a graphic and extremely valuable lesson that we can apply to our more effective use of Creative Mind power.

First, with all the many and varied uses to which electricity has been put, its nature has not changed. Second, these uses were potential before man discovered he could tap this power. Third, the *expressions* of electricity as light, radio, television, X ray, computer, etc., are determined not by their nature alone but by the instruments man created as outlets for that nature. As man expands his understanding of electrical power, his ideas expand. As these ideas become definite, definite results follow. Ideas, not power, produce the amazing developments.

In the application of Creative Mind power the parallel is direct. The nature of the power remains unchanged no matter how it is used, and all action is potential in it whether man knows this or not. The particular expressions of this power, as the individual's manifold experiences, are determined not by the power but by the subjectified ideas in the individual's consciousness. The unformed power that is to express as your experience takes the form of the mold you give it. It cannot enlarge the mold any more than electricity can enlarge a ten-watt bulb. But as electricity lights a hundred- or a thousand-watt bulb just as easily as a ten-watt, so the power of Mind fills with ease the greatest specific idea of good that you can accept.

Do not fret that being specific will limit you. It may limit a particular demonstration, but remember that Edison's first lamp was very limited—yet look what it started! Ideas expand with each demonstration, and the expanded idea produces an expanded good.

Meditate until the idea of the good you desire is clear, definite, and specific in your thought. Then incorporate it in your treatment. Treatment is the means by which one subjectifies and accepts the idea he desires to experience. When you give a treatment, you definitely, constructively, actively state, sense, know some specific good.

TREATMENT

My Life Declares the Glory of God

The universe displays the intelligence, creativity, and order of the Infinite Spirit. In all and through all Spirit is expressing Itself. With wonder and awe I open to the realization that this applies to me. What Spirit is, I am. What the universe displays is mine to display also.

Divine Intelligence illuminates my consciousness and

guides my every choice toward richer expression of life. My decisions to act on these choices are clear, crisp, and definite. The Law of Mind, honoring my decisions, displays health in my body and prosperity in my affairs.

Creativity surges in my thought as new, fresh, vital ideas. The joy of giving them expression today releases all the yesterdays of both triumph and defeat, and reveals the future as simply a promise of even greater good to be. Order, "heaven's first law," insures the correct sequence of my creative ideas, choices, and decisions. The harmonious flow of all my activities and relationships is the natural result, and the glory of God is displayed in my life.

* * *

Making the Demand

One of the great lessons evolution teaches is that there is an intelligence in Life that responds to demand. It produced legs when creatures of the sea grasped for the land. It developed wings when the earthbound reached for the sky. It designed exquisite camouflage for those seeking protection from their predators. Nature on all sides abounds with proof of intelligent response to subconscious demands, which obviously the above are.

The same Intelligence responds to conscious demand. Witness the fantastic development in chemistry, with the host of synthetic materials; in physics, with the yield of atomic power; in electronics, with television, computer "brains," and control of spacecraft. Men asked questions, they sought answers, they knocked at the doors hiding nature's secrets. In response to their demands, miracles burst forth. Furthermore, there is overwhelming evidence of direct and immediate response as healing and as creative inspiration, flowing into expression, through artists, architects, composers, writers, and inventors.

It is the nature of Intelligence or Universal Mind to respond to demand by producing a corresponding expression. How and why Mind functions this way is a matter of theory. That it does is a matter of fact, which is the all-important point to the person who would make practical use of this unlimited potential.

Note the common and therefore essential elements in the above-mentioned conscious demands. First is the desire for a new or different experience, expression, or manifestation. Second is an idea, at least a general one, of the form the fulfilled desire will take. (Note that the result usually far exceeds your expectations.) Third is a conviction or faith that results will appear. *Desire, idea, conviction*—when your demand encompasses these three, the response is inevitable.

Important for beneficial results: The qualities *involved* in the desire and idea will *evolve* in the result. Eliminate all but those of a life-giving, positive, constructive nature consistent with the general good of all.

"Ask, and it shall be given you; seek, and ye shall find; knock, and it shall be opened unto you" (Matthew 7:7).

Make your demand and trust Mind to respond.

TREATMENT

I Rejoice in My Divine Right to Choose

The Spirit of God is my life. The Mind of God is my source of wisdom. The Law of God is the action by which the substance of being becomes my experience. As an individualization of Spirit, I am imbued with the attributes of Spirit. Selection and initiative are inherent in my nature. I am endowed with the privilege and responsibility to choose my thoughts. I choose wisely, knowing that the Law impersonally executes my decision.

Aware of my divine authority, I look without fear at the conditions and appearances in my world. To each I declare: "You have no power to make me indulge in negative speculation, unhappiness, or sorrow. There is one power and one cause in my life, and I use it for good."

I rejoice as I select excellent thoughts to embrace in my consciousness. I delight in filling my mind with creative, constructive, life-giving ideas. I am buoyant with the sheer joy of knowing that, by choice, I create the fulfilling life that God intended.

* * *

Your blueprint for tomorrow exists in the beliefs you subjectify today. A clear and definite specification of what you desire is a prerequisite to its appearance in your experience. The next step in "making it happen" is to picture, or imagine, the *best* that can manifest, knowing that Mind will produce this or better.

CHAPTER 6

AMPLIFY

Amplify your acceptance of the fact that your desired good is a completed reality in Mind.

Amplify your acceptance of the fact that your desired good is a completed reality in Mind. Feed the power of faith into it. See yourself living in your demonstration. Appreciate it, love it, enjoy it in your imagination. Let it become so real to you that the last vestige of doubt vanishes. Creation is finished; your desired good is alive. You freely release it to the marvelous action of the Law of Mind, knowing that the Law will produce this desire or something better.

Acting As If

The decision has been made to sell the old house and buy a new one. An experienced real estate agent knows that the sooner the mental and emotional ties to the old place are released, the more quickly it will sell. Wisely, then, you begin to act as if it were already sold. Mentally you move out of the old and into the new. To strengthen this mental image, you clear out all the accumulation of odds and ends from the closets and top shelves. You get rid of everything that is not appropriate for the new home. You even begin to pack what you do not need for everyday use.

Now you move your emotion into the new home. Visualize friends basking in the warmth and cheer of the fire in the fireplace you have always wanted. Feel the rising appreciation for the convenience of a modern kitchen and the luxury of plenty of room and an extra bath. Augment this by refusing to indulge in either complaint or nostalgia about the old quarters. Because you have "acted as if," you will be startled by the smoothness, ease, and rapidity of the actual transition to your new home.

This illustrates both a principle and a technique applicable to every desired experience. The fulfillment of a new idea requires the mental and emotional release of the old which it is to replace. Infinite Mind can give you only what you are prepared to receive.

When you have decided to move into a new experience and have given the idea to Mind, ask yourself the following questions: (1) Which of my thoughts, feelings, and habit patterns are incompatible with the new idea and must be released? (2) If this were to happen within the next twenty-four hours, what would I want in readiness? (3) What will living in the new experience be like? Now carefully think through to the answers. Next, use them to let go of the old and accept the new. You cooperate with Mind by acting as if the desired result is inevitable. And so it *is*.

I Am Patient

God, the Infinite Presence of Life, Intelligence, and Creative Power, is the one source of all that Good implies. The significance of this sublime truth expands in my conscious awareness. The One Presence is present where I am. Around and within me is the very source of the good I seek. My mind is centered in the intelligence that knows the way. I am one with the Creative Power that can bring it to pass.

I honor the Mind that transcends my intellect. I accept the fact that It knows the order, sequence, and timing of my unfolding good. This completely clears any tendency to be impatient. I am not anxious, for I trust the perfect action of Mind. I do not attempt to force or manipulate, for I have complete faith in the Law of Growth. I do what is now before me to do, with the calm assurance that this is an essential part of my growing good. I wait patiently on the Law in joyous expectancy of the full bloom.

*   *   *

The Eye of the Mind

The dense fog and black night had reduced visibility to zero. In spite of this, and the rugged, rocky coast only a few miles to the port side, the freighter steamed on full-speed ahead. The captain stood watch in total darkness on the bridge, quietly, confidently navigating the ship. Instead of straining his physical vision in a futile attempt to penetrate the impenetrable, he gazed at an instrument similar to a television screen. The picture of the coastline was sharp and clear. Distances to the danger points showed also. A ship appeared on the screen headed our way. Still there was no cause for alarm. Observations of its movement on the screen determined its course four miles to starboard. The captain was using the invisible eye of radar to pierce the limits of human vision and guide his ship safely through the fog and darkness.

Available to you is the "invisible eye" of Mind that can pierce the limits of the intellect and the five senses. It can be used to chart a safe and direct course to your destination through the darkest circumstances and the foggiest conditions. To use this "invisible eye," three steps are necessary.

First, realize that, at the subjective level, your mind is one with the Universal Subjective in which is known every force, thought, or potential condition that could conceivably affect—favorably or adversely—the manifestation of good you desire.

Second, direct your subjective mind to chart the best course to your goal. (Being the best course, it will not interfere with anyone's good.) Subjective Mind, because it is *subjective,* does as you direct and brings to bear upon the problem its unlimited intelligence.

Third, take a tip from the captain who darkened the bridge that he might better see the screen. Shut out the world of appearances along with the judgments thereof, and give your full attention and confidence to the intuitions that arise from the deeper levels and all-inclusive scope of the Big Mind.

"I will instruct thee and teach thee in the way which thou shalt go: I will guide thee with mine eye" (Psalm 32:8).

TREATMENT

My Vision Is Clear

The Spirit of God is all-pervading. The Infinite is forever the Infinite. Yet the One is eternally taking form as the many. On all sides It manifests. Within me, as me, *It is*. In this simple truth there is no distortion. In this realization my vision is clear. Any fear of looking within or without dissolves.

Within my consciousness the light of my clear vision illuminates the self God created. Shadowy images of inadequacy have vanished. No specters of failure, sickness, or death remain. I know who I am: an individualization of the Living Spirit, born to give It unique expression. This purpose of being is supported, sustained, and supplied by the love, intelligence, and power of Mind. My mission is to bear witness to this truth in thought, word, and action. I accept this mission in confidence and joy without reservation.

I view the world around me in this light. In people, places, and circumstances the Divine receives my recognition. I see through threatening appearances to the inner reality of ever-present good. I declare this good, and my declaration reveals it.

*   *   *

Dynamic Vision

Have you wondered why dreams come true for some people and not for others; why some consistently arrive at their goals while others falter, lose their way, and sink into a morass of discouragement? Have you charged this to *luck?* Actually, there are mental and spiritual principles involved. If these principles are used correctly, the dream of hope becomes a dynamic vision of faith that rises over obstacles, threads through interference, and moves to fulfillment.

Four factors are necessary to convert an ephemeral dream into a vital vision: (1) Belief that what you desire can happen; (2) realistic acceptance of the fact that life moves forward; (3) courage to face challenges; (4) patience to take one step at a time.

Begin by realizing, *"This can happen to me."* For years space travel was believed to be impossible. One day a dreamer, glimpsing the yet unfathomed reservoirs of intelligence, power, and natural resources, said, "This can happen." At that moment the "impossible" became possible; the dreamer became a man of action. Think of the creative intelligence, power, and resources of Infinite Mind. Know these are available to you because you are a center in Mind. Then say of your dream, *"This is possible. It can happen to me."*

Next accept that *life moves forward.* Your coming experience will not be patterned after yesterday. It will be fashioned in all the freshness of tomorrow. To any anxiety

over the unknown say, "Be still. I trust the Mind that
directs my path."

Courage to face challenges grows with recognition that
you are in partnership with Mind. Working *through* you
is Mind's unlimited capacity to solve whatever problems
you meet. This realization carried you beyond courage
into an eagerness that grasps challenges "as a strong man
to run a race."

Patience to take one step at a time is the flowering of
faith in the action of Mind, which forges each link in the
chain of circumstances leading to your goal.

As you accept your desired good as *possible* and move
forward, facing challenges eagerly, taking each step *patiently* and confidently, your dream becomes a vision of
reality.

TREATMENT

My Vision Expands

God is the infinite potential of my life, the inexhaustible
essence of my being, the unlimited intelligence of my
mind, the unquenchable light of my spirit. The promise
of greatness is implicit in the image and likeness created
by God as me. I was born not of the flesh but of spirit, not
to bondage but to freedom. I am intended not for medioc-
rity but for the radiant expression of God's glory.

Knowing, then, that limitations are none other than the
boundaries of my own vision, I loose the bonds of cap-
tivity. I lift my eyes above human bondage to the high
peaks of Divine Potential. In every area of my life—health,

finance, vocation, relationships, service to mankind—old boundaries are breached by the released inner light. I behold all things new.

I trust the purpose for which I was born. God's wisdom, love, and power guide, sustain, and support me. On the wings of my expanded vision I rise to greet the golden opportunities of the years ahead.

*   *   *

Patient and persistent visualization of receiving and experiencing your desired good helps you to build confident expectation and acceptance of it. Repeated picturing of your desire as a completed reality in Mind readies you to take the final step of creative thinking—rejoicing in and glorifying the action that is manifesting your good.

CHAPTER 7

GLORIFY

*Glorify, appreciate, rejoice in the action that you know
is manifesting your good.*

Glorify the action that you know is taking place. Say to yourself, "Living power is now flowing into the vital seed I have planted in the nurturing soil of Mind. I rejoice that Infinite Wisdom is guiding me step by step in the unfoldment of my good. My appreciation of the great Laws of Mind and Harmony grows. I glory in the Spirit, Life, and Mind of God around and within me."

To appreciate means to be fully conscious of, to be aware of, to be alive and sensitive to. Through your contemplation of any aspect of creation, you grow in appreciation of the Creator; you become more *conscious* of the one Creative Power; you grow in *awareness* of the fact that this Power acts through Law; you become *alive* to the one vital Substance out of which are made both man and the universe; you are *sensitive* to the Intelligence that guides the entire creative process from cause to effect. You awaken to the startling truth that the one Power is eternally seeking expression through *you*. Appreciation blends your consciousness with the very Spirit of Creation. In this vital awareness you know yourself to be a unique and necessary instrument by means of which will manifest yet un-dreamed-of good.

Gratitude

A clear understanding of the significance and function of gratitude is essential to the successful application of the principles of creative meditation. Let us begin by clearing two prevalent and false concepts.

First, when we are told to be grateful for the good we have, too often the implication is "just be glad things are not worse." This is basically negative and, while better than complaining, denies the limitless potential of life. Second, much that has been said and written concerning thanksgiving to God conveys the idea that God hungers for man's praise and appreciation and, not getting it, will cut off the supply of good. This is attributing to the Divine a human tendency—an age-old practice of "making God in man's image and likeness."

Creative meditation recognizes God as the omnipresent source of *all*, "giver of every good and perfect gift, giving liberally (and equally) to all." The infinite givingness is limited only by the vessel that receives it. The use of atomic energy, for example, is limited only by man's ideas of the reactors and other mechanisms that release this as power. Faith is the mechanism through which the energy of Mind is released. Ideas are the vessels that measure the portion of infinite good expressed in your life.

The function of gratitude is twofold. First, it focuses your attention on the good already manifesting in your experience, rather than its opposite. Thus it enlarges the vessel measuring your good, because Mind power flows toward and increases the object of your attention. The second function is illustrated in the story of the feeding of the multitude. In the face of great need, Jesus gave thanks that the need was met—and it was.

Treatment for the manifestation of a particular good is closed by a definite declaration of gratitude for that good as already received. This establishes the attitude of expectancy and faith that releases the energy of Mind into your chosen channel.

TREATMENT

Appreciation Expands My Abundant Good

The miraculous action of Mind is active in me and through me. Appreciation of Its unique creation, which I am, expands my awareness and consequently my cooperation with It at all levels. I marvel at the creative Intelligence that designed and built my body and that, at this moment, is forming new cells in every nerve, organ, and muscle of this incredible vehicle I use. My rejoicing in this continual renewing action of Mind sweeps from my consciousness all attitudes that could in any way interfere.

I stand in awe as Mind molds outer garments for my thoughts and brings them forth as new experiences. Wonder of wonders, my ideas take form through the same marvelous process that formed the sun, the stars, and my body. Aware of the beauty and simplicity of this truth, I entertain only life-giving thoughts. I think in terms of wholeness, harmony, productiveness, and joy. The action of Mind moves me into a richer, fuller, more abundant life.

I glory in my growing appreciation of God, acting in and through me.

*   *   *

Release

A vital step in treatment is releasing your desire to the Law of Mind. The omission of this step can block your demonstration. This step and how the Law acts is uniquely illustrated by dialing someone in a distant city. Dialing connects you with an amazing piece of equipment called the "sender." The *sender* stores in its "memory" the area code and your friend's number. When you have completed dialing, it goes to work with singleness of purpose, combined with the knowledge of what to do and how to do it, to complete your call.

Suppose you are calling Chicago from San Francisco. The sender tries a direct line. If it is busy, it routes your call over whatever circuit is available. Your subsequent conversation may be via Portland, Seattle, and Minneapolis, or via Phoenix, Atlanta, and New York. You know nothing of this. The sender completes your call using whatever means are necessary—and does it easily and efficiently *if* you do not interfere. Should you become impatient or worry that you may have dialed the wrong number and hang up, the sender does not complete your call.

The Law of Mind operates much like the sender. You

give instructions as to your desire. Mind receives these instructions, stores them in memory, then proceeds, with singleness of purpose, combined with the knowledge of what to do and how to do it, to produce the desired result in your experience. This it will do, using whatever means are necessary, *if* you do not interfere. If you yield to the often strong temptation to dictate to the Law the means by which your good shall be accomplished, you usually block your demonstration. On the other hand, as you contemplate the fact that you have no more certain knowledge of the right means by which your good shall come than you have knowledge of the right circuit for your phone call, you are willing to let go and trust the intelligence of the great Law of Mind to complete your demonstration in perfect time and order.

"Commit thy way unto the Lord [Law]; trust also in him; and he shall bring it to pass" (Psalm 37:5).

TREATMENT

I Bear Witness to Truth

The Spirit of God is forever designing new forms. The Law of God is forever bringing them to pass. The universe is forever declaring the glory of this creative action. As one of God's creations, I am a divine idea destined by the Spirit for Its own fulfillment.

Since the Perfect cannot create imperfection, my purpose is clear. It cannot be other than full, rich, and complete expression of the One Life. I refuse to accept half-measures, half-truths, and half-gods. I accept nothing less than the full measure of my divine inheritance. This includes health of body, mind, and activity; prosperity of endeavor; radiance of life; fullness of joy; and an ever-increasing revelation of that which I truly am.

With no reservations, I commit unto the great Law the end to which I was born and the means to it. With thought, word, and action, I bear witness to the truth of my being and am freed into expressions of life that declare the glory of God.

* * *

The Principle of Praise

One of the most valuable lessons science teaches is that success begins with a sound knowledge of fundamental principles. This is true in every line of endeavor. The real musician is well grounded in principles of composition, harmony, and technique. The architect must know principles of construction and design; the salesman, basic principles of selling. Those who try to use ready-made formulas mechanically may get some results, but sooner or later they run into conditions where formulas will not work, and they are lost. Whereas the one who knows his fundamentals can apply them to any condition or situation. This is particularly true in the application of Mind power, and is the reason fundamentals are emphasized in these lessons.

Praise is a specialized use of Mind power. In the myriad of books on gaining friends, securing cooperation, and influencing people, hundreds of formulas have been given for its use. The formulas produce "lip praise" and yield only superficial results—unless the underlying principle is tapped. The key to this principle lies in the Latin root of "praise" (*pretiare*, to prize), which is also the root of "appreciate." "Appreciate," while meaning "grateful for," also means "to increase in value," as "depreciate" means "to decrease in value." That which we *sincerely* appreciate and praise increases. Praise integrity, ingenuity, cooperation, creativeness in another or ourselves, and the expressions of these qualities amplify. This is true because Mind power always flows into and increases the object of our attention.

While the principle of praise is important to successful human relations, it is even more important in our relationship with God. This is emphasized by the fact that the Bible uses the word over three hundred times. Why? What increases when we discerningly praise God? Certainly not *God,* for it is self-evident that the infinite cannot be expanded. We increase our *awareness* of God and the God-qualities of life, wisdom, power, and love flowing in and through us, and therefore the expressions of these qualities in our lives. No wonder the wise have always said, "Praise God and prosper in all things."

TREATMENT

I Delight in the Law

The action of God's laws in the universe, as order, is glorious to behold. The paths of the planets, the flowering of a seed, the fury of a storm all eloquently speak of laws man did not make and cannot change. Yet the laws of gravity, growth, and release of power obey me implicitly as I first obey them. Truly through law God gave man potential dominion over the world.

I accept the responsibility that goes with dominion. I appreciate the responsibility that goes with dominion. I appreciate and respect the Law of Mind that establishes me in authority in my world. As surely as the seasons roll, action follows thought. From the inward man the outer man appears. I choose with wisdom and love the thoughts I entertain, for they shape the inner man. I glory in the immutable action of Law that translates them into experience.

Health, harmony, peace, and prosperity flower for me because I plant their seeds in my heart. Permanence of principle is my security for I delight in the law of God.

*   *   *

Appreciation, praise, and thanksgiving finalize your attunement with Infinite Mind and its definite law of creative action. To glorify Mind's action is to joyfully recognize the manifestation of unlimited good awaiting your acceptance of it in consciousness.

SUMMARY

Each time you follow through with the seven steps of creative meditation you move to a permanently higher level of consciousness. You are more attuned to the presence and nature of God. You are more secure in your true identity. You are more aware of your unity with all life and all people. Furthermore, as you continue in this process, good beyond anything you now imagine flows from your God-center into your world. It is a blessing and a benediction to all, for it bears witness unto the truth. Thus does your purpose for being move into ever-increasing fulfillment.

Suppose, however, that after a reasonable period following your treatment there is no indication of desired results. A basic principle in every field of applied science is this: "Whenever the solution to a problem balks, go back to fundamentals and check your procedure." This is particularly important in the application of creative thought principles. Instead of letting deadly doubt creep in, check to be sure your treatment includes all seven fundamental steps. The absence of any one can block results. The presence of all assures results. Ask yourself the following questions:

1. "Do I fully accept the principle of Omnipresence as infinite Life, unlimited Power, transcendent Intelligence, inexhaustible Supply, and all-encompassing Love, to the total exclusion of all belief in any opposing force?" The conviction that God is all good eliminates fear that an outside condition or person can thwart the particular good you desire.

2. "Do I believe in my heart that I am constantly surrounded and infused with this Presence?" Realization of your unity with God dissolves the delusion of separation from the source of your good.

3. "Do I truly recognize the presence of God in all creation as the fundamental unity of being?" When you can say with inner conviction that in the Infinite Spirit, Mind, and Being, you are one with all people, your sense of unity expands in consciousness. It dissolves fear and resentment and establishes you in the Law of Harmony.

4. "Do I thoroughly understand the great Law of Creative Power: that it acts to produce in my experience what I consciously and subconsciously accept, and that this is the *only* way it can act?" "With what measure ye mete, it shall be measured to you again" (Matthew 7:2). Perception here clarifies that God can only do for you what God can do *through* you. But remember, it is done with "good measure, pressed down, shaken together and running over."

5. "Is the good I desire defined clearly enough to be recognizable when it appears?" A vague treatment produces vague results. Meditate until what you truly want

is clear, then state it. Being definite is not restrictive.

6. "Do I feel that this good already belongs to me, and have I released the 'how' of its manifestation?" Acceptance is essential. Treat until you *feel* it, then *let go*. Outlining the "how" is limiting. Leave that entirely to the intelligent action of the great Law, and you will rejoice in your demonstration.

7. "Am I generous in my praise, appreciation, and gratitude that Infinite Wisdom is unfolding my good in orderly sequence according to the Law of Mind?" Thanksgiving that the good is already manifest further invokes the Law of Attraction, bringing forth all things necessary for its perfect expression in your experience.

How long should you persist in the practice of following these steps of creative meditation? Continue until your desired good has become an actual part of your life, remembering that to the Infinite Mind there is nothing too great nor too small for consideration, one thing is not more difficult than another, and all persons are equally deserving of good.

Stopping Power Leaks

The Power of God can do *for* you only what it can do *through* you. Understanding this fundamental principle is essential to the effective use of creative meditation. In it we discover why the potential of abundant life in everyone is limited in expression. Consider this illustration.

Fred connected the hose and turned on the faucet. To his surprise only a trickle of water came from the sprinkler. A check of the faucet indicated full pressure. A check of the hose revealed a number of leaks through which force and flow were being dissipated. Fred repaired the breaks, and the sprinkler worked perfectly. The faucet represents the unlimited source of substance and power to which you are permanently connected; the sprinkler, any constructive, creative idea you desire expressed in your life; the hose, your consciousness through which substance and power flow from source to expression.

If your desired good is not manifesting, check for and repair power leaks in your consciousness—thoughts and feelings that divert divine energy to no good purpose. The major leaks (fear, doubt, hate, anger, self-pity, etc.) that can divert the entire flow are obvious, and volumes have been written on how to handle them. To detect and stop other leaks, remember the principle: "Power flows toward the object of your attention." Then ask yourself: "Is my attention on idle or negative talk (my own or another's); gossip (simple or pernicious); purposeless reading or televisoin viewing; silent, victorious debate with some imaginary opponent; past mistakes; hard luck; etc.? If so, *"Is this where I really want the power?"* The choice is yours. If the answer is "no," withdraw your attention, and you stop the leak. In the case of idle chatter or gossip, one need not be rude; simply change the subject, remain politely silent, or courteously leave.

As leaks are repaired and power increases at the point of your desired good from a trickle to full force, you understand why John Ciardi said, "A man is finally defined by what he does with his attention." You might even agree with Simone Weil, "Absolute attention is absolute prayer."

Cultivating Consciousness

Farmer A complained that the soil of his farm was unproductive. Each spring he would rough up the surface of the hard ground, buy good seed and scatter it. Each fall, regardless of his high hopes, the harvest was always sparse. Finally, in despair he sold the land. The new owner, Farmer B, deep-plowed the ground, pulverized the hard lumps, applied soil conditioners to prevent their reforming, planted the same quality seed, and reaped a harvest that was the envy of the neighborhood.

There is One Mind common to all, with universal characteristics of intelligence, creative power, and law. In the indivdiual, this subjective mind can be conditioned and, through fear, doubt, resentment, belief in limitation, etc., become unproductive. It can also be reconditioned into the "soil" in which your ideas will grow to fruition.

Farmer A is like the man who has valuable ideas but does not understand the nature of Mind or the condition of his own subjective. He operates at the surface level with schemes, salesmanship, and willpower, continually frustrated by stunted results.

Farmer B is like the man, also with valuable ideas, who realizes that he needs a healthy environment, so proceeds to cultivate his consciousness. With fingers of faith, wisdom, and courage he reaches deep into hardened habits of thinking and feeling, breaking up the lumps he finds there:

Example of Master Plan for Creative Meditation

I desire *a new home*

Specifications:

Qualities *Harmonious, peaceful, comfortable, beautiful, hospitable*

Form *light spacious rooms, ranch-type, reasonably priced, convenient location, soundly constructed*

Outline of treatment used covering the seven steps of creative thinking:

1. *There is one Mind, one Life, one Spirit everywhere present.*
2. *I am surrounded with this Mind and am one with It.*
3. *I am one with all people; my fulfilled desire is beneficial for all.*
4. *Universal Mind acts in perfect order & harmony to manifest my desire.*
5. *The new home I expect is already overflowing with love, beauty, joy.*
6. *I see myself enjoying my new home with family & friends.*
7. *I rejoice that my new home is a completed reality in Mind; Thank God!*

How will I feel when the demonstration is complete? _____
Overjoyed!

Date treatment began *Sept. 10*

Date demonstration was completed *Nov. 7*

Notes _____

Fear, which would crush life from an idea;

Belief in limitation, which would shut out the flow of power;

Doubt, which would choke any sprouts;

Resentment, which would alienate cooperation.

Now he applies vital conditioners:

Confidence in the presence, power, intelligence, and Law of Mind;

Appreciation of Life;

Genuine goodwill toward all.

In this porous and positively conditioned consciousness, a creative idea sinks easily to the subjective, where it draws freely upon the unlimited resources of Mind. Quite naturally, the law of growth produces the full-blown manifestation of all the potential in the idea. Friends of this man probably call him "lucky."

PART TWO

Applying the Seven Steps of Creative Meditation

INTRODUCTION

Spiritual mind treatment is based upon the fact that right where you are God is. This fundamental reality is of the utmost importance to your life because *it is your life*. God as Mind is always responding to your subjective belief by establishing this subjective belief in your world. The thoughts upon which you dwell consciously, repeatedly, take root in the subconscious and form the subjective patterns that Mind automatically translates into experience. What you think of yourself as being, you are in the process of becoming!

The following discussions and treatments are designed to help you use creative thought to become the positive expression of your divine potential. Each consists of statements that announce various facets of this potential. As you study and state the spiritual mind treatments, think of yourself as *being* what you state. Thinking thus, you initiate the process of *becoming*. As you continue consciously, definitely thinking in this way, the creative thoughts take root, new patterns form at the subjective level, and Mind produces corresponding expressions in your experience.

CHAPTER 8

LIFE

Health, Wholeness, Balance, Vitality

Spiritual Vitality

A healthy body is a prize possession. Through our five senses we contact the outer world and the people in it. If the body is not healthy, the senses are not operating at peak efficiency and we are missing part of life. Health is the natural rhythm and tune of the body. Sickness is a result of some discordant vibration that breaks the rhythm and distorts the tune.

To understand this fully we must realize that man is more than physical, more than mental. You say "my body"—a statement of possession by something greater than the body. You say "I think"—recognition that *you* use your mind—*you,* a person beyond your mind and body . . . a *spiritual being.* This is the basic truth of our nature, and when we think and act from this basis, and only then, we are in tune with ourselves and with life. This is the level from which all life flows. Here we contact vitality at its very source. With a strong awareness of this spiritual vitality and an eagerness to express it in every phase of our daily lives, we find that mental and physical health follow naturally.

It is when we step down from this higher awareness that we run into trouble. Regret, worry, and fear throw our inner worlds into a state of turmoil that saps our physical strength until the body is easy prey to any disease that happens along. This inner weakness, this susceptibility to disease, referred to by doctors as "low resistance," is the primary cause of sickness. The medical profession is generally agreed that a person of "high resistance" is immune to ordinary ills.

High resistance, then, is a requisite of physical well-being, and it results when spiritual vitality, with all its life-giving power, flows freely from the depths of our being. Spiritual vitality floods the mind with light and drives out the dark specters of guilt, resentment, fear, envy, and self-pity. It races through the blood with tingling energy, rejuvenates the cells, and restores the body to the image of wholeness and health that Mind designed.

TREATMENTS

I Feel Great

There is one Mind, Creator of heaven and earth, Sustainer of the invisible and visible universe, God of all flesh and of the spirit that dwells therein. There is one Unity of Being expressing in infinite variety. Life is Its principle. Order is Its law. Dynamic balance is Its action.

Permanently clear in my consciousness is this truth: I am one with the Unity of Being. My mind, emotions, and body rest on Its principle, move through Its law, express in Its action. My health is ordained and maintained by the creating Intelligence that individualized me out of Itself.

Knowing the inner reality of health, I cannot be deceived into believing that conditions (temperature, humidity, altitude) or foreign substances (germs, pollen, virus) can cause dysfunction. The Sustainer of my body adapts it to all conditions. The God of my flesh vanquishes all invaders. Life, springing from the Source, flows through the mental-emotional-physical instrument of my being, with rhythmic order, into dynamically balanced action. I feel great!

I Arise in a New Dimension

The Eternal Life of the Infinite Spirit is the resurrecting power. In the perpetual forward flow of its living stream, old forms fall away to arise anew, full, fresh, and vibrant. This is the glorious way of Life. It is my song, and I sing it with the bursting joy of a spring day.

The life of God welling up from the center of my being dissolves all thoughts, feelings, and actions that burden and crucify. I watch the old beliefs of a self separated from its Source disintegrate as icicles melt in a warm spring sun. And as the water carries food to the new forms of the earth, the living water of Spirit nourishes the new person.

I give full sway to the resurrecting power. I am renewed in body, mind, and purpose. Life tingles in my veins. Inspiration illumines my thoughts. Wisdom directs my way. Harmony and love govern my actions. I delight in the new dimension of life to which I have arisen.

*   *   *

The Reality of Health

Hans, an artisan woodworker, gazed at an exquisitely carved table. A piece here and there had been broken and lost. The question was how to design and carve pieces to restore those missing. Obviously in a work of art such as this, innovations would be grotesque. Only an exact duplicate of the original pattern would be right. At the moment Hans could not worry over the problem. He was too caught up in the beauty and grace of that which he beheld.

As so often happens when one becomes absorbed in a work of art, Hans began to sense the spirit of the creating artist. Soon, in his mind's eye, he saw the form of the missing pieces. Each one fitted harmoniously into the vision of wholeness that was now clear. The problem was solved. Only the mechanics remained. Find the right wood, in grain and shade. Fashion it to the form so vividly perceived. Then fasten the pieces in place.

You, as a student of creative thinking, know exactly what took place. An idea is never lost in Mind. Once created, it always *is*. The original design of the table had never changed. It existed above time, place, and circumstance. Hans, by letting the spirit of what he saw infuse his consciousness, looked through the visible form to the invisible, changeless reality.

Now consider health in this light. The Infinite Artist could not design an imperfect body, any more than our other artist would design a broken table. The idea in Mind of your body is that of a whole, vibrant vehicle for the spiritual being that you are. This divine idea is your true health. It can never be lost or broken. It *is*, above time, place, and circumstance.

Furthermore Life, flowing in every atom of your being, is forever seeking to manifest this idea as *your* body. Let it. Cooperate by contemplating the miraculous design of hands, eyes, ears, feet, the process of converting food into new vital cells at the rate of millions per minute. Let the spirit of the Creating Artist infuse your consciousness. Rejoice in the changeless reality that your health is.

TREATMENTS

I Thank God for My Health

God is All in All. Spirit designs, Mind produces; and the Universe declares the magnificence of this action. What is true of the whole is true of the part. That part of the One that I call my body has Spirit for father and Mind for mother. It was born not of the flesh but of the will of God for the glory of God to manifest as wholeness.

I accept my responsibility for establishing and maintaining my consciousness in line with this wholeness. I dissolve all thoughts that are not in accord with the fullness of Life. I release all emotions that distort the harmony of Being. My past mistakes are thus cleared, and God heals their consequent discord and pain.

I rejoice in the healing process as it reveals the design of Spirit. I marvel as Mind produces a renewed body. I use this beautiful instrument for increasing expression of Good. Light has broken forth in my awareness. Love flows as my emotion. I thank God for my health.

I Appreciate My Body

Spirit created me out of Itself to be a unique expression of Itself. Spirit designed my body as a whole, healthy vehicle for Itself as me. This wondrous creation is self-regulating and self-renewing, completely equipped to fulfill its purpose. The light of the designing Intelligence glows in every one of its trillions of atoms. Literally this physical instrument is a bundle of atomic energy, bursting with life.

As I contemplate the truth of this glorious creation, my vision beholds only light in form. Dissolved by this light are all the dark specters of disease, impairment and old age. Spirit knows nothing of these and neither do I.

Radiant health is the normal standard, and I accept what is normal. I expect to feel vital and strong, and I plan my activities accordingly. I think, feel, and act as the Infinite intends I should. Creative ideas fill my consciousness. Love of life flows in my emotions. Only good expresses in my actions. I richly appreciate my wonderful body through which all this happens.

*　　　*　　　*

What About Doctors?

The starting point of every treatment for healing is the recognition, fundamental in creative thinking, that there is *one* healing agency—the Creative Intelligence and Power that built the body—Divine Mind. Sound evidence involving every disease known to man proves the premise that

Mind can heal, unaided by material ministrations. This raises the often asked question: "What should be my attitude toward doctors?"

Certainly it should begin with an open-minded appreciation of the fine work done by dedicated men in this field. A helpful idea comes from the great Canadian physician Sir William Osler: "The doctor binds up the wounds. God heals."

Suppose you are treating for someone (John) who is ill or injured, and a doctor is handling the case. Say to yourself: "The healing intelligence and power of Divine Mind infuses John's entire being. This same intelligence pervades the consciousness of the doctor, the nurses, and everyone attending this case, guiding every thought and action toward the physical manifestation of the healing that already is complete in Mind."

Recently a case in which a man with a severe spinal injury was to undergo a delicate and difficult operation was treated as above. Following the operation the surgeon reported: "From the moment I was handed the scalpel through the entire procedure, it was as though my hand were guided by an unseen hand. Never before have I known so clearly that I was an instrument of something greater than I. Furthermore, I knew from the beginning that all was well." The patient healed in a fraction of the normally anticipated time.

Now some may ask: "Since Mind alone can heal, why call a doctor at all?" The answer lies in a cardinal principle of creative thinking: The primary focus of treatment is *not* on the *means* but on the desired *result and* the fact that the limitless intelligence of Mind knows what to do and how to do it. When, as a consequence of treatment, the "how" unfolds, cooperate with it. If a doctor is drawn in, recognize this instrument of Mind while continuing to know and trust the One Healing Power.

The Life of God Radiates in My Body

God is the Source of all being, the One cause, design, and action in all and through all. I live in proof of Divine causation, for the creativeness of God brought forth my body. Every part of this miraculous instrument evidences designing Intelligence. I marvel at the hands that do my bidding, at my feet that have carried me unmeasured distances. I think with wonder and delight of touch, tasting, and hearing. Beyond wonder are my eyes, receiving light and transmitting images to my mind.

As my appreciation of creation daily grows, I know without doubt that the design of this holy temple is without flaw. The life within it, the Life of God, is a fountain bubbling up and flowing fresh into every cell, nerve, organ, and function. The healing, renewing action is continuous, and thoughts that harmonize with this action fill my consciousness with peace, gratitude, beauty, and joy.

As the Source of my being radiates through me and from me, my body glorifies God.

I Am Emotionally Balanced

God is Power, God is Love, God is Mind. Made of the essence and likeness of God, my true nature is Divine. Unlimited Power is mine to use. Infinite Mind, as my mind, directs my use of Power. Divine Love, radiating in my consciousness, imbues my desires with the highest motives.

I refuse to be governed by the spirit of fear or any of its attendant emotions. Feelings of hostility, resentment, or bitterness are dissolved by my understanding that they are only shadows arising out of past conditioning. I give no thought and no power to negative feelings, for they are not a part of my true nature. I think, speak, and act according to the highest good I know, and warm, confident emotions inevitably follow.

I am centered in Power, Love, and Mind. Emotionally I am dynamically balanced. I like myself because I know who I am. Goodwill flows from me at all times to all people. I rejoice in the increasing harmony of my inner and outer life.

CHAPTER 9

LOVE

The Qualities of Love

How elusive is the secret of love, the love that reaches out to everyone everywhere! We yearn to experience a true kinship with all people. Something within us responds to the beautiful concept of universal brotherhood. We realize that love would lift our lives above pettiness, egotism, and selfishness; we acknowledge it as the one thing that will save humanity from self-destruction—yet the feeling often eludes us.

In longing for this perfect love now, we are wishing for something that can come only through development—we are wanting to be at the mountaintop without making the climb. We move toward this great goal by beginning where we are to express some of the qualities of love, for in every such expression we expand toward the higher ideal. But what are these qualities?

Since there is individual life, there must be a Universal Life. Since there are individual expressions of love, there must be a Universal Love. We can learn much about this perfect Love by observing its actions. We see its manifestations all around us, the sunshine and rain given freely to the just and unjust alike, the abundance of good poured forth for all to enjoy, the wonderful laws of nature that apply with impartial justice to all.

One of Love's greatest gifts is the power of choice, the power that makes us people and not robots. We can accept or reject, and if we refuse to respond to life's richness, the Infinite Giver is not hurt. If we fail to rise to the beauty of a sunset, our insensitivity is not the Artist's loss. Universal Love is impersonal until it finds a heart that awakens to it. Then it becomes individual and personal, warming and glorifying existence.

In all this we find the basic qualities of Love in action: a giving forth of goodwill, giving without judging the receiver, allowing complete freedom of thought and expression, never binding or coercing but letting each find his own way. These, then, are the qualities we must begin to personalize. In so doing, we will be taking the first big step toward our ideal of loving and being loved.

TREATMENTS

Love Blesses My Life

I love the Presence of God that surrounds me. I love the Spirit of God that indwells me. I love the Mind of God that fills my consciousness with creative, constructive, expansive ideas. I love the Law of God that clothes these ideas with form and brings them forth as experience. I love the Love of God that lifts my whole being to the level of harmonious action. I love the Joy of God that infuses my life with radiance and beauty. Therefore I know that all things work together for good.

Especially do I realize this today. I look back on every experience my human mind has labeled bad, unfortunate, or even disastrous. I affirm and accept the blessing from each one, as did Jacob of old, and let them all go. From each apparent mistake of the past, I absorb the valuable lesson and release, completely, all else. Freed into a greater love and appreciation of God, I greet each new day with joyous expectation.

I Accept Myself

By Divine design was I formed. By Mind's intent was I sent forth. I am a spiritual citizen of a spiritual universe moving among spiritual people in the unfoldment of the supreme spiritual purpose of Life. My role is to fully express my Self. To this end I was endowed with life, the unlimited capacity to love, and the torch of truth that burns eternally at the center of my being.

I accept myself. I release from my consciousness all that is unlike what I truly am. I free myself from feelings of inadequacy, guilt, and fear by recognizing that they stem from the misconception that I am something other than God-created and God-sustained. Perceiving the falsity of their foundation, I give such negative feelings no power and let them evaporate.

I accept the purpose to which I was born. I enthusiastically embrace every opportunity to let life express. Love motivates my relationships. The light of truth makes crystal-clear my direction. The universe is enriched by the expression of God's intent as me.

*   *   *

Love in Action

Many have declared love to be the greatest healing, prospering, creating power in the universe. This *sounds* good, but is it true? It is a beautiful theory, but will it prove out in fact? The only way to *know* is to test the theory in the laboratory of our own lives.

If a test is to be run in a laboratory, it is necessary to define the area to be covered and the elements involved. For our purpose we are thinking of love that can be expressed in *all* relationships, not just intimate ones. The elements must be those that we can *choose* to think about and act upon regardless of feelings, likes, or dislikes. For this experiment, seven elements and declarations for their use are suggested:

Patience—to accept a seed's own rate of growth. I will seek to express this toward others *and* toward myself.

Kindness—I will seek to know the *truly* kind action, rather than that which simply eases my feelings, and then do it.

Generosity—my attention will be on how I can give of myself rather than on what I can get.

Humility—I will be teachable, and what I do in love I will do in secret if possible.

Courtesy—consideration and thoughtfulness shall govern my attitudes and actions.

Unselfishness—I give up the "right" to be mad, sad, hurt, and resentful. I will not blame others for the way I feel.

Sincerity—I will think and act with integrity and in good faith.

Since we actually live in Mind, our thoughts are cause to our experience. The experiment begins, then, at the level of cause. Meditation upon each of the elements will throw additional light on its meaning and bring it to life. As elements of love come to life in your consciousness, you begin to act upon them. Each action will in turn strengthen them in your consciousness.

TREATMENTS

I Witness the Truth

Man is the image and likeness of God. God is spirit. Man is spirit. Spirit is perfection itself. Imperfection cannot flow from perfection any more than contaminated water can flow from a pure spring. God could not make an imperfect man.

Knowing this, I cease to pin false labels on others and on myself. A person may be suffering in a problem and be blinded by it, but I am no longer blinded. All labels such as alcoholic, diabetic, cripple, aged, retarded, murderer, thief, and liar are false, and I now erase them from my consciousness. The problem is not the person. The person is spirit. This separation is clear and permanent in my understanding.

I am now free to handle any problem, my own or that

of another, from the standpoint of Truth. All barriers to communication and understanding are dissolved because I meet, talk to, and think about persons, spiritual beings, and not problems. The believer and the belief are parted. I witness the Truth.

I Am Teachable

The Infinite breathed Itself into me for a purpose. Since I am an incarnation of Spirit, my purpose is to express the qualities of Spirit. Thus the full potential of life and creativeness, of love, wisdom, and power, is my divine birthright. Furthermore, my instructor in the fulfillment of my purpose and potential is none other than God—the Light of my being. My mind and heart are open and receptive. I am teachable.

The inner Light radiates to every facet of my experience. As it is reflected to my heightening awareness, I understand in a new way. I see mistakes in their true perspective. They tell me in graphic terms: "The Law of Mind is immutable." I bless them for the lessons learned and let them go. The stress of self-recrimination is released. My consciousness is free and clear. I am responsive to the inner Light. It illuminates and magnifies the thoughts and feelings that accord with my purpose and potential. The truth is clear, the way is straight, life is fulfilling—because I am teachable.

*　　　*　　　*

Walking in Love

We are all familiar with the recorded events of the Resurrection of Jesus almost 2,000 years ago. Whether these events be literally true or not, we will all agree that Jesus was a Master of Life, not of death. If we look at his teachings, particularly those magnificent ideas expressed in the Sermon on the Mount, we find that his focus is on the here, not on the hereafter.

All of us realize that we have something within us that is greater than we are. What makes Jesus unique is that he recognized in this inner greatness the truth that he was made in the image and likeness of God. You and I may not have come into this full realization as yet. But the same mind is within us that was within him. You and I have within us the potential of transcendence, of life more glorious, even as did he.

If you and I can keep this in mind as we meet people on the everyday plane of our experience, realizing that no matter what mask they put on, no matter how low in the human scale they may appear, they are misrepresenting themselves, we are beginning to give the "resurrection" idea meaning in our own lives. If we are alive and alert to the fact that within others, as within us, is this greater glory—if we are prepared always to give a word of recognition, of encouragement, to others as well as ourselves— we will be resurrecting life in a true and great sense. We will be *walking in the divine spirit of Love.*

In this awareness of the indwelling God, we resurrect our thinking, transcend our former selves, and transform our world every day we live. What better way to pay tribute to the Master of Life?

TREATMENTS

Love Expresses Vitally through Me

I am immersed in Love. My ears hear it in the song of the birds. My eyes revel in its color and beauty. I taste it in the succulent apple, inhale it from the rose. In the handclasp of a friend it tingles through my whole being. Truly One Love permeates the universe. The Spirit of God is above all, around all, and within all.

I am *aware* of Love, the Love of God, at the center of my being. There is no room in my consciousness for beliefs, no matter how widespread, that deny this reality. Thoughts of inharmony, misunderstanding, and disappointment in others or myself I bundle up and cast into the living flame. With a glorious sense of release, I watch them evaporate into their native nothingness.

I rejoice in Love. It vitalizes every area of my experience. I express Love with wisdom and joyfully accept its expression from others. The world around me is blessed and harmonized because Love expresses vitally through me.

I Declare the Loving Self God Made

Spirit is universal. The Infinite centers at every point. The Presence of God *is*—One in all, all in One. What God is, is where I am and what I am. Love, Life, Mind, Power,

Substance, Joy are centered in me as the essence of my being. My body is the temple of God.

Aware of my true nature and indwelling authority, I silence the voices of the earthly self that tell me what I am not. The whimperings of fear and the whinings of self-pity cease. Ramblings of fault-finding and criticism halt. The whisperings of inferiority I dismiss as nonsense. The mutterings "You are inadequate," "You will fail" I laugh out of existence.

I know my divine potential. I think the loving thoughts God thought of me in the beginning. I speak my words of power. I am upright and honest. Health and harmony are habitual in my body and affairs. Prosperity is the order of my activities. Love, as goodwill, governs my relationships. My spiritual integrity is inviolate. I declare the loving Self God made.

CHAPTER 10

LIGHT

Ever Available Guidance

All of us know what it means to want and need guidance. And this need is not new to our confusing age; apparently it is as old as man. The Bible records many appeals for guidance, and it is filled with assurances that guidance is always available.

Awareness of this unfailing availability is the starting point of making divine guidance a powerful force in our lives. When we really consider the Intelligence that keeps the universe functioning in perfect law and order, we cannot doubt that the Mind that directs the path of the planets is more than able to direct the paths of our individual expression.

From this basic premise we move to the next point: How do we tune in to this infallible guidance? We do this by withdrawing attention from the world of effects and turning within to the Cause from which all effects flow—Mind. Here at the fountainhead we find fresh, clear ideas, ideas that lead us along the shortest and happiest route to our goals.

The lives of many outstandingly successful people have been built around the practice of starting the day with meditation, a quiet period in which they simply listened to the Big Mind. Then, vitalized with new ideas, they moved into the activity of unfolding those ideas in their experience.

As children we learned the value of the simple formula of running the best possible race: *Get ready, get set, Go!* By beginning the day with a regular period of meditation, we apply much the same technique. We *get ready* by becoming quiet and in balance; we *get set* by alerting ourselves to guidance from the Big Mind; and then we *go* into the pursuits of the day. Jesus made a practice of such inner preparation by withdrawing from the multitudes of people and activities. For example, "when he was set" (Matthew 5:1) he proceeded to give his Sermon on the Mount.

We can be sure always of following the right course of action if we will (1) be aware of the divine guidance ever-available; (2) trust it; (3) use it.

TREATMENTS

God Is My Guide

From the high vantage point in Mind, both the beginning and end of my venture are in focus. The One Intelligence perceives where I am, my desired destination, and the path between. Just as with a seed, every increment of growth, from germination to fruition, is foreordained, so Mind sees clearly every detail of the route leading from where I am to where I will be.

Knowing this, I release all human speculation pertaining to outline, plans, developments, steps to take, and people to contact. I dissolve all anxious concern over how future action will unfold.

I am now open and free to receive guidance emanating from all-knowing Mind. With complete confidence, I follow directions. Plans unfold with the ease of a growing plant. The next step is obvious, for it follows in order the one just taken. I am drawn to the right people at the right time, for their good as well as mine. I rejoice that the process of achievement is effortless because God is my guide.

My Guidance Is at Hand

God as Mind is total intelligence. In Mind there are no unanswered or unanswerable questions. A universal order precludes loose ends. The answer exists simultaneously with the question, the solution with the problem, the means with the purpose.

I am a center in Mind, not an isolated thinker, thinking alone. I am aware of this, and lack of *conscious* knowledge will never again delude me into believing that needed knowledge is unavailable. Whatever I must know for a particular purpose, at a particular time, is known by the Infinite Knower at the center of my being. This realization eliminates all worry over not knowing consciously in advance.

My consciousness is now a flexible, uninhibited instrument of Divine Mind. Into my thoughts flow creative constructive ideas of good seeking expression by means of me. Answers become clear; solutions unfold; means manifest in orderly, timely sequence. I am inspired, guided, and directed by the intellect-transcending wisdom. I rejoice, as toward each purpose I move with ease and confidence.

*   *   *

How to Solve a Problem

If a situation blocks our progress we have a problem. The solution removes the block. We move on. The succession of problems followed by solutions is the way life proceeds to greater expression. A sound problem-solving technique is therefore essential to success.

Dr. Land, inventor of the Polaroid camera, in an interview referred to such a technique, the one used by every successful scientist. He said, "If you are able to state a problem—any problem—it can be solved. If the problem is clearly important, then time dwindles and all sorts of resources which have evolved to help you handle complex situations seem to fall into place, letting you solve problems you never dreamed you could solve." Outlined here for application by you, as a creative thinker, is this effective approach:

1. *Clarify the problem.* Illness, lack, discord in relationships, buyer resistance, or whatever the situation may seem to be the problem. *It is not.* It is a condition *caused* by the problem. Illness is a condition caused by inner conflict, lack of money by a belief in scarcity, buyer resistance by an attitude focused on selling rather than serving, dis-

cord by misunderstanding, and so on. As the cause in consciousness is clarified, the problem is clearly seen as inner
conflict, belief, attitude, misunderstanding, etc.

2. *Affirm that in Mind the solution already is.* To the
Infinite Intelligence the solution is simply the other half
of the problem. Declare that Mind in you knows how to
harmonize the conflict, is the Source of abundant supply,
by Its very nature serves, sees the common purpose above
misunderstanding, and so on.

3. *Activate the Power of Mind* by focusing attention
exclusively on the desired results.

4. *Cooperate calmly and unhurriedly.* As Mind unfolds
in perfect sequence outer elements of the solution, your
part in the action becomes clearly evident. Rejoice in each
step even though you may not yet see all the pieces in
place.

As you clarify the problem, affirm the solution in Mind,
activate the Power, and cooperate, "you solve problems
you never dreamed you could."

TREATMENTS

The Solution Is Now

The Mind of God is the guiding, directing, creating intelligence of the universe. Obviously it is greater than any
problem that can possibly face me this day. Thus the solution I need for any particular problem already exists in
Mind. It is a right solution that will bring forth good for
all concerned because it is governed by the unity of Life
and the law of harmony. Furthermore, this solution is

instantly available to me since the One Mind is the Mind in which my mind is centered.

The light of this truth now flows into every area of my consciousness, dissolving completely all anxiety, apprehension, and any belief that an obstacle can block my way.

My complete attention is on the solution that is now unfolding in my conscious awareness. Expectation of guidance and direction opens every channel of my being to the flow of Divine right action. Strength, faith, and courage fill my heart. Peace floods my mind. I move forward with confidence, knowing that the solution is now.

Divine Mind Reveals the Answer

The Divine Mind of God is infinite intelligence. It encompasses all. It infuses all. It is all-knowing at the point where I am. Divine Mind at the center of my conciousness knows the answer even before my human thinking recognizes or becomes baffled by the problem. Knowing this, I cease my mental striving and let my awareness come alive to inner knowing.

God now thinks through me the ideas that lead me out of the darkness of confusion into the light of understanding. I am no longer troubled by the appearance of a difficult condition. I worry no more over what others may do.

My attention is not on the problem but on the answer! The answer I know is complete and laden with good even beyond my hopes. Its elements unfold and are revealed to me in perfect sequence. I accept with thanksgiving. I re-

joice in the right action that is even now bringing forth
the good, the true, and the wonderful.

*   *   *

Intuition Is Real

There is a light within each of us that, if followed, will
guide unerringly, as the gyroscope keeps a ship steadily on
its course. This light, often called intuition, is much like
an inner eye, a faculty that transcends time and space and
reaches out beyond the limited range of our physical
senses to bring us knowledge otherwise unavailable to us.

Regardless of what we are doing, we have decisions to
make. Intuition leads us to the decision that is best for us
and everyone else involved. It inspires us to say the right
thing, to use words and expressions that promote understanding. It helps us chart the best possible course.

The first step toward using intuition is to become aware
of it, to recognize that such a power exists. We must open
our minds to the fact that we have direct access to Infinite
Wisdom, from which intuition comes. As we seek intuition
and expect it, our awareness increases.

The second step is learning to trust implicitly, and this
comes as a result of growth. When a theory, such as intuition, is unproved, believing is difficult. So we accept the
theory on a trial basis and put it into the laboratory of
our own lives. When it begins to work and proves to be
true, our faith grows. We learn to trust because we *know*
from our own experience.

The third step is to develop a recognition of guidance

when it comes. In some instances it is a definite picture of what to do; in others, specific words may come to mind. But more often it is a *"sensing"* that a certain thing should, or should not, be done or said. With practice we develop a sense of "inner touch" that helps us distinguish between actual guidance and groundless fancies. This *touch* increases in sensitivity with our sincere desire for truth and our recognition of its spiritual source.

Intuition is a reality, but we must *use* it in order to reap the benefits of correct decisions and right actions, to experience the joy, exhilaration, and inspiration that come with increasing spiritual awareness. As Ralph Waldo Emerson taught, a man should learn to detect and watch that gleam of light which flashes across his mind from within, more than the luster of the firmament of bards and sages.

TREATMENTS

I Am the Light of My World

Light is an integral part of the nature of God. This divine light is knowing beyond human knowledge, is understanding beyond human perception, is wisdom beyond human judgment. This is "the light that lighteth every man that cometh into the world." This is the light at the center of my consciousness now.

Quietly I let the light radiate into every area of my consciousness. Where there was the darkness of fear, now there is the light of faith. Where there were shadows of indecision, now there is the light of divine knowing. Where there were gloomy negatives of distrust and resentment, now there is the light of loving understanding. Where there was confusion, now there is the light of the wisdom that sees beyond appearances.

Inner knowing clarifies my human knowledge. True understanding lifts my vision. Divine wisdom guides all my decisions into right action.

I am the light of my world. I let the light shine now unto the perfect day before me.

I Cooperate with Mind

Divine Mind encompasses and permeates all. As creative intelligence It is active at every point in the universe. As unlimited knowing It holds the true answer to every question, the right solution to every problem. This applies specifically to me. I am centered in Mind. I am one with the action and knowledge of Mind. The guidance I seek, the activity I need, are right at the point where I am.

I release all straining to calculate from appearances. My thoughts and emotions relax. Calmly and quietly I contemplate the beautiful truth that the ideal solution *is* now. Furthermore, every step from where I stand to the happy conclusion is known in perfect sequence. The beginning, middle, and end are one in Mind. Without reservation of any kind, I fully accept this in both mind and heart.

My consciousness is clear and open to the creative intelligence in action. I am keenly receptive to the flashes of intuition that guide my way. With joy and great expectations I cooperate with the wisdom and action of Mind.

CHAPTER 11

PEACE

Serenity Can Be Realized

There are so many distractions in this uncertain, struggling world that the feeling of inner peace is rarely experienced. Yet most of us consider it one of life's greatest prizes. A business person says, in the mad rush of the afternoon, "This evening when I have finished work I will have some peace." A parent burdened with debt sighs, "When I am free of these obligations I will know peace." A member of a large family complains, "With so many people around, peace is impossible . . . if only I could be alone!" Yet a lonely person thinks, "Only when I have found loving companionship will I know peace."

We may have in mind a desired condition that we think would bring peace. Yet experience warns us that we hope in vain. Often we escape from an irritating situation only to find ourselves in another one more annoying. Sometimes we retire to a quiet, restful place hoping to feel peaceful, yet that subtle inner restlessness remains. We pursue peace and do not find it. However, we have found it when we did not seek it: when we were achieving some worthwhile objective; when we "made up" with someone we had been angry with and the warm feeling of friendliness flowed through us, sweeping out malice, envy, and self-righteousness; when we, after repeated efforts to solve a problem had failed, turned within for guidance and found the answer.

Inner peace is never born of outside conditions. It comes when we have harmonized our thoughts, feelings, and actions with the inmost core of our being—the Over-soul—the Divine within. Until we have begun to do this there can be no peace, because there is war in the inner world. Our reason fights our desire, and our actions are the poor, ragged children of this conflict.

Peace comes only when we stop looking to things, people, and outer conditions to bring peace and happiness, and throw ourselves unconditionally upon our own inner resources. Immediately the conflict ceases, all the forces of our being work in harmony, and we know the serenity that comes to the one who has found his true Self.

TREATMENTS

I Live in Harmony

The harmony of Infinite Mind is an obvious verity. God cannot be opposed to God. The universe is in dynamic balance. Thus every expression of the One is designed by Mind to be in fundamental harmony with every other expression of the One. As a creation of Infinite Mind I am a Divine Idea, infused with the principle of harmony.

Within me is the vital seed of a creative, constructive, life-expanding relationship with every person, place, and thing.

The light of this inherent truth floods my consciousness, clears my vision, and illumines my way. Any belief that another can be against my good, my ongoing, or my growth is dissolved. No obstacle can stand in the path of my progress. No circumstance can block the unfoldment of my Divine potential. Gone are all attendant fears and frustrations.

My every forward movement flows in accord with the One and therefore with all. I live in harmony. I know the peace of God. From my heart radiates goodwill toward everyone everywhere.

Wisdom Illuminates My Quiet Mind

Mind is the all-encompassing One in which I am. From this Divine center in me, wisdom—revealing right decisions—flashes as intuition. It transcends opinions and judgments of the intellect, mine or those of others. Half-truths vanish in the light of this wisdom, which *is* truth.

Aware of the wonder of Mind, I let my human opinions lie quiet. Judgments are released. The static of outer news is stilled. Preconceived ideas of what people will say and do are dissolved. Calmly I let go of all previously held convictions. That which is true, by its own nature, remains. That which is alien to truth departs. My total consciousness is now open and receptive to the flow of transcendent wisdom.

Every idea that comes to my attention moves instantly into true perspective. All its facets are fully perceived and understood. At each crossroad of decision the *right* way is clearly seen. With quiet confidence I select it. Ensuing action flows in completeness and harmony guided by Divine Mind, with which my mind is one.

*   *   *

The Secret of Harmonious Relationships—
True Communication

Though I speak *with the tongues of angels, if I do not communicate, my words are empty symbols.* True communication is the key to peaceful relationships: international, national, and personal. This is true because communication means knowledge-in-common; knowledge-in-common means understanding (though not necessarily *agreement*); understanding eliminates suspicion; where there is no suspicion, fear is dissolved; and where fear is dissolved, amicable relations are easily established.

The principle of communication is One Mind. This is valid because the One Mind and, therefore, all knowledge, is common to all people. Why, then, are there difficulties in communication? It is because the knowledge shared in common is at the subjective level. The problem is that of bringing it to the conscious level. The student of creative thinking has the solution because he knows that Mind responds to desire coupled with faith.

Everyone desires to be understood, but this must be matched with the desire to *understand.* Combine this with faith in the action of Mind, and communication, with all its attendant benefits, is established.

I Understand and Am Understood

In the Infinite One, I am. In the all-encompassing, infusing Spirit, I live. In Divine Mind, my mind is. As I am, so are all people. We exist in basic Unity, uniquely express the same Spirit, share the Mind common to all. I open my consciousness to the significance of this great truth. My thoughts rise to a new level of what it can mean in all my relationships.

As I consciously recognize the presence of Mind in everyone, I am intensely aware of this in all my communications. The one who speaks to me and to whom I speak is in and of the same Mind. There are no barriers to understanding. There is no misinterpretation, no confusion. The messages are clear, the meaning comprehended. Divergent views expressing inherent uniqueness as well as points of agreement are understood and respected. The letters I write and receive are in the same spirit of true communication, for in Mind there is no distance. I rejoice in understanding and being understood.

Divine Equality Governs My Relationships

I have faith in the eternal fatherhood of God and the brotherhood of man. As children of God, all are joint heirs of Mind. There is no great nor small in the divine equality. Everyone on the face of the earth is co-equal with me in sharing the infinite potential of being.

I share with all people the love of God. Everyone responds to this love. The respect I give is given to me. I am unified with the best and finest in every heart and mind. With all, I climb the upward path toward complete expression of the inner Man, which from the beginning has been perfect.

The magnificent impartiality of God-presence illuminates my consciousness, dissolving all that is unlike it. I let go of my human way of thinking, and I let God think and love through me. I deal not with human beings but with the expressions of God. God loves them by means of me, and this love is reflected in our relationships. The divine equality blesses all.

*   *   *

The Process of Peace

Behold the order, harmony, and beauty of growth! From seed to bloom, Creation's hand is sure. In perfect order a single cell divides to multiply. From one the many come to gather into galaxies that blend in harmony and flow to fill the form conceived in Mind before the seed was born. As root and stem and bloom, we call it beauty. As thought, as life, as action we also call it beauty. Is not this whole process, without a single discordant note, the personification of peace?

The Peace of God is not inaction. It is Life flowing with divine order into beautiful and fulfilling expression.

To know *this* peace, enlist the process of growth. Let the idea of good you desire lie quietly in Mind while Divine Intelligence designs the orderly, harmonious plan of unfoldment. In perfect season, inner growth pushes outward and your living good flows into form. Cultivate it with patience. Water it with faith. *Let* it grow. Marvel at its beauty. As you do these things, God as Peace moves in your mind, your heart, and your affairs.

TREATMENTS

I Express the Qualities of Dynamic Peace

The Spirit of God formed me out of Its own essence; thus the harmony, order, and balance of the Infinite One are inherent in my true nature. I am unified, guided, and maintained by those qualities of God. The flow of my life is channeled into expressions of dynamic peace.

Divine harmony unifies my consciousness with the Source of Life. Consequently my thoughts are attuned only to ideas that are life-giving, love-inspiring, and good-producing. I have no affinity with their opposites.

Divine order guides my decisions at every step in every venture. I always choose the direction of movement—physical, mental, and emotional—that is in accord with the highest and the best. Any tendency to settle for less is eliminated.

Divine balance maintains a healthy relationship among all of my activities. Work and rest, creativity and play blend into one harmonious whole. Harmony, order, and balance establish the dynamic peace that blesses and prospers my life.

I Know the Truth of My Country

There is One Mind, in which all divine ideas are established. There is One Power carrying these ideas into manifestation.

In Mind is the divine idea of this nation, conceived in justice and liberty, and established on the fundamental truth that all people are created equal. Inherent in the idea is the general welfare and common good, and therefore, according to the Principle of Unity and the Law of Harmony, the individual welfare and good of every man, woman, and child.

Divine love radiating from the center of this idea now infuses the heart of every individual in every community, every city, and every state, dissolving all unlike itself. The unity and harmony in the idea dissolves all partisan proposals made to the leader of our country. Infinite wisdom, flowing by means of the idea, surrounds and permeates his consciousness, guiding his every decision. The One Power carries each of these divinely directed decisions into right action. I rejoice that God's idea of my country now manifests.

CHAPTER 12

POWER

Your Power Center

Webster says that the word "practical" implies success in meeting the demands made by actual living. The spiritual approach to life is practical because it enables the individual to meet successfully the demands of life on the inner plane as well as in the outer world. It provides the means by which you fill out your physical needs, yet at the same time partake of the only substance that can satisfy your inner hunger. The spiritually oriented individual is the one who is continually drawing closer to his own God-center in the growing realization that from this center flows his entire life experience—on all levels.

As you move closer to your God-center, you become increasingly aware that Jesus knew whereof he spoke when he said, "Seek ye first the kingdom of God and *all* will be added unto you." This has nothing to do with theology, doctrine, or creed. It has to do with the spiritual reality which you are, and your awakening to the fact that within you is a power greater than you are. The God you are seeking is God at the center of your being. Knowing this, you draw closer to this center in consciousness, and from it comes the strength, the wisdom, the power, and the love you need to meet successfully the demands of your outer life.

One of the very practical results from the spiritual approach to life is that you find that you have to spend less and less time rearranging your world because you are in harmony with the source of the life that is flowing into your world and creating it. You discover that the closer you attune yourself to God, the Infinite Good within you, the more your world rearranges itself to be in harmony with this Good, the supply that always exceeds the demand.

The spiritually aligned person has the power and peace that comes only from wholeness and self-integration. With Spirit as your center, you are a force for good and a blessing to your world.

TREATMENTS

The Presence of God Is the Power of My Life

The presence of God around and within me is the source of my being, the light of my life, and the power of my consciousness. There is no other source, light, or power. All my experiences form as light and power flow from the one source through my beliefs and anticipations.

As a spiritual being, I know my birthright to be the freedom to choose what I will believe and anticipate; thus no one else can interfere with my good. I fear none.

No condition or circumstance can bind me. The very way in which light and power flow through me is my salvation, for I alone select my thoughts.

I wholeheartedly accept full responsibility for what I think, choose, decide, believe, and anticipate. I think of the healthy, the harmonious, and the abundant. I choose the way that produces good for all. I decide on right action. I believe in my goals. God prospers and blesses me as light and power flow through the exhilarating, fulfilling activities I anticipate bringing to pass.

I Am Alive with Life

All life flows from one fountainhead—God. Therefore the essence of life is the nature of God. The life of God, living Itself as me, is what I am. I individualize the One Life.

Every atom, cell, organ, and function of my body vibrates with divine vitality and is tuned to the harmony of wholeness. Thoughts of disease, sickness, and death are not in accord with life and have no power over me. They are false concepts arising from the world of appearances, and I reject them. Health is the reality of my body.

Health is the state of my mind. Living ideas from Infinite Mind flow into and fill my consciousness. I am constantly aware of their powerful impulse to manifest greater good through me. I am ever alert to the inherent intelligence guiding these vital ideas in their orderly, successful unfoldment. Each fulfilled idea is a step on my upward path of spiritual evolution. I rejoice in the life of God expressing Itself by means of me.

*   *   *

Don't Limit Tomorrow

There are four ways by which we limit the potential greatness of tomorrow: regretting past mistakes, reliving yesterday's glories, believing in the limitation of advancing age, and projecting our present weaknesses into future conditions.

Regret carries the burdens of guilt, condemnation, and self-pity, which combine to inhibit the flow of God's creative power. Learn from mistakes and let them go.

Reliving the "good old days" is, in essence, saying that the creativity that produced the glorious yesterday is incapable of producing a more glorious tomorrow. This is a denial of Life's expansive principle.

The number of years since you were born has nothing to do with your capabilities as a child of God. You are now and forever on the path of progress.

There is a subtle tendency to project today's conditions into yet unborn experiences. This results from failing to realize that you are growing spiritually. Tomorrow you will have *greater* ideas and a *higher* consciousness of God than you have today. Knowing this, leave tomorrow unbound and free to be gloriously new.

TREATMENTS

Today Is the Only One That Counts

Yesterday is dead. Tomorrow with its rich potential is yet unborn. I have only *today* in which to live.

I know this intellectually, but let me see clearly the full import of this fundamental reality. *Right now* is the only time I can think; it is the only time I can feel; it is the only time I can set the Law of Mind in operation. *Right now* is the only time I can turn my thoughts to the Indwelling God, the only time I can experience its warm Inner Presence.

What a wonderful realization! This moment is the most important in my life. What I believe, think, and feel at this moment *is* my life—and by the Great Law it will unfold in my experience. Therefore I open my heart to the Power, the Love, and the Wisdom of God in me now. I accept the Universal Good which is mine—now. I give thanks for the growing awareness that I live only in the forever-glorious today.

I Am a New Action

God, the one creating Principle, unbound by any precedent, is the renewing action of my total being. Spirit, quickening my consciousness, is forever lifting my vision to higher levels of perception and understanding. Mind, moving in my world of thought, constantly presents greater ideas to replace those no longer appropriate. Life, as fresh as this moment, flows through my body. Revitalization is a perpetual process. Renewal is a continuing activity.

I cooperate with the action of God in and through me. I am completely willing to release all I have outgrown. The past has no fascination for me. I let it go. I am a now person in a now action.

I glory in the higher, wider vision of unlimited potential. A fuller sense of unity, harmony, and beauty greets my expanding awareness. I embrace heretofore unseen creative ideas, and intriguing, rewarding experiences unfold. That which is becoming is greater, richer, and more fulfilling than anything I have known. I delight in God, the ever-new action of my total being now.

*   *   *

Imagination and Faith

The Bible abounds with references to the planting and the harvest, because this process is such a striking analogy to the Law of Mind in action. We *can* improve our lives, not by willpower but by thinking in a new way. A superior kind of thought seed, sown with faith in the creative field of Mind, cannot fail to yield a superior harvest.

An understanding of the relationship of faith to creative imagination is important to the effective application of spiritual principles. *Creative imagination* is that function of mind that forms or pictures an idea with such clarity and feeling that the idea comes alive in consciousness. *Faith* is a feeling belief, "the substance of things hoped for" (Hebrews 11:1).

Compare the "live idea" to a seed, and the "substance" of faith to the soil. In a seed the plant is a living image, which remains dormant until the seed is submerged in the soil. Substance then flows into the seed and is converted by the livingness thereof into the outer form of the plant.

The life-giving power of your imagination literally conceives the ideas that you bring into the imaging room of your mind. You endow them with life. They become living entities. But, like seeds, they must be filled with substance. Knowing this, you pour into your *desired* ideas the substance of your faith and watch the invisible images push outward into tangible experience.

Every morning the sun rises on a new opportunity to change your life for the better in every way. Do not waste today lamenting the limited harvests of yesterday. Now is the season to plant anew, knowing that the same Law that produced meagerness or discord can now produce bounty and harmony. Train yourself to think about what you want instead of what you do not want. Dedicate a period each day to creative meditation and spiritual mind treatment. Direct your energies into specific aims. Bring to life your images of good. Feed them with the substance of your faith. Then let the Law of Growth work for you.

TREATMENTS

I Express My True Nature

The Infinite Spirit *is*. Forever creating out of Itself, It is both the formless and the form, life and body, cause and effect. All is *one*. This truth permeates my consciousness. What Spirit is, I am. The nature of Spirit—creative, boundless, and free—is my nature. The essence of Spirit—life, love, and light—is the essence of my being. Through the law of Spirit, thought takes form. By this law I am in authority in my world.

As Spirit I cannot stop creating. Thoughts I entertain are, by the action of law, continually moving into expression. Knowing this and my freedom of choice, I invite into my mental home only ideas in harmony with the essence of my being. I firmly refuse entry to their opposites.

My consciousness is filled with living ideas that flow into vital, radiant, and prosperous activity. The essence of love imbues every creation with harmony of action. Only good for all concerned manifests through the great law. Light in every thought illuminates all expressions of the boundless Spirit which I am.

I See and Move Directly

The intelligence of Divine Mind in me transcends my intellect. It knows how to plot a direct course and lay out a highway for me to travel from where I am to where I want to be. There are no errors in its calculations. As a man lost in the wilderness seeks a high point from which to see across the terrain, so do I abandon my human attempts to think my way through the conditions that block my path. Instead, I rise to that high point in Mind where I join the highway. Here I see directly.

The Power of God in me is the only power there is. As I set foot upon my envisioned highway, I do so in the sure knowledge that there is no cause for "accident" or delay. The One Power moves me directly and easily.

Serene in the certainty of my destination, I am relaxed. The people I meet are friends. The conditions I encounter hold only good. The highway I follow is a joy.

CHAPTER 13

BEAUTY

Expressing Your Real Self

The face on the television screen was distorted by a wavy motion that continually changed the shape and proportions. Obviously this was not the way the singer really looked. There was interference of some kind—in the transmission, in the atmosphere, or in the set. The difficulty was not in the origin of the picture. Nor was it in the screen, because sometimes the picture would be clear and in focus. The cause of the distortion had to be in the *medium* of expression.

Your Divine identity—your God-created Real Self—is that which in truth you are, to give, do, and be. Now, the purpose of Life must be to fulfill Itself. Thus the prime purpose in each of us must be to give full expression to the Real Self.

How can we tell when the expression is true and when it is distorted? In the case of the television image, we recognize the distortion because we know the general characteristics of head and body and that they do not change from moment to moment. In the case of the Self we have no such criteria. We must look to qualities that are intrinsic in a Divine idea and therefore inherent in the Self: wholeness; vitality of spirit, mind, and body; internal harmony; love—all the means necessary for complete expression and progressive unfoldment.

Look at a particular experience that is appearing on the screen of your life. If the Divine qualities (and none of their opposites) are present, you know that what is appearing is an undistorted expression of your Real Self, an individualization of your true and unique identity. If any of these qualities is distorted or lacking, what must be changed to clear the picture? Not your Real Self, for it is the flawless creation of God. Not the screen of life, for it is simply a reflection.

The distortion has to be in the *medium* of expression—and that medium is subjective mind. The distortion is in the form of subjectified misconception, mistaken belief, prejudice, and obsession.

You clear the distortion by the consistent use of creative meditation and spiritual mind treatment—and enjoy expressing your Real Self.

TREATMENTS

I Have Courage to Be My Self

The Spirit of God is the one creative action, forever bringing into being unique expressions of Itself. Man was formed in Spirit, by Spirit, of Spirit; imbued with life, love, wisdom, and power; and endowed with the capacity for unlimited expression of his divine nature. The Self-contemplation of God brought me into being as a unique individualization of Itself.

I am neither an accident nor a mistake. I am not patterned by either heredity or environment. Human ideas and race thoughts do not squeeze me into a mold. I am not limited by world opinions, and I am not bound by any former false beliefs.

I allow full freedom to the true idea of me to be, in and through me, the person God intended. I rejoice in the uniqueness implanted in me. God's idea of me determines my activities. I give forth freely that which I alone have to give. Life, love, wisdom, and power uphold me as I have the courage to be my Self.

I Know My Purpose and Fulfill It

There is one infinite, creative, sustaining intelligence and power: *Mind*. Being infinite, It is perfect. Being creative, It creates in the fullness of perfection. Being the sustaining power, It powers Its creation. As a creation of Mind, I am a divine idea inherently perfect and inseparable from the power that forever sustains me.

Growing awareness of this truth radiates into my every thought and feeling. Any misjudgments labeling me inadequate or inferior are eradicated by the testimony of my inner Self. Any beliefs linking me with limitation of any kind are shown as false by the Light shining from the center of my being.

Awake to my true nature, I am clear in my prime purpose: to let the divine idea blossom in every phase and facet of my life. This purpose now dominates my consciousness. Inner perfection expresses through my thought, word, and action. The sustaining power of Mind renews, revitalizes, and carries me onward. The glory of God glows from the divine idea which I am.

*   *   *

Integrity

Integrity is defined as "soundness . . . the state of being complete or undivided." The priceless quality of integrity can be yours through your determined right thinking.

Life is a continual process of deciding how you will think about each successive condition or idea that comes to your attention. If you choose the limited or defeatist human point of view, you move toward disintegration. If you choose the standpoint of spiritual perception, viewing every challenge in the light of the spiritual power, intelligence, and law that you can bring to bear upon it, you are in the process of integration.

Jesus said, "If thine eye be single, thy whole body shall be full of light." As you dedicate yourself to the wonderful goal of integrity, deciding to appraise and handle each unfolding experience from the center of God-consciousness within you, the integrating light of inner peace and renewal shines ever brighter through everything you say and do. Soundness of mind and body is yours to know. Completeness is yours to enjoy.

I Accept My Divine Nature

The Indwelling God is my Heavenly Father, for the kingdom of heaven is within me, and all that I can ever need or desire is already potential in this inner realm. I knock at the door of this magnificent inner realm, and because I have knocked it is opened unto me.

In this divine awareness I dwell in the perfect consciousness of God, and my outer life unfolds in patterns of beauty and abundance. The great love and givingness of God flows out into my world, bringing balance and harmony to my activities.

I let the creativity of God in me fill my consciousness with its divine ideas. I let the intelligence of God guide my way. I let the wisdom of God instruct me along the path. With a glad heart I follow these instructions, for I know they lead to the experience of growth, happiness, and fulfillment. The glory of the inner realm reveals itself in my life. I accept the truth of my divine nature with rejoicing.

I Travel God's Highway

Order is heaven's first law. Sequence is sovereign. Beginning, middle, and end are one. Mind knows inception, pathway, and goal as a single unified movement. The highway from my present point of departure to my chosen destination is ordered by God's law of unfoldment. It is aligned by divine intelligence, constructed according to universal principles, and paved with the promise of harmonious progress.

I am consciously attuned to the guiding, coordinating Spirit of my being. Every journey, of every kind, that I make—be it for pleasure, business, creative expression, or spiritual growth—is enfolded in the indwelling and omnipresent wisdom of Mind. I am in the right place, at the right time, functioning in right relationships with people, places, and conditions. Hills and curves that obstruct distant vision do not bother me. My way is "the way of the Lord," and I trust it.

My destination is certain, and on God's highway I travel easily, safely, and happily toward it.

*   *   *

What's Your Hurry?

To hurry is to rush ahead out of balance. Examples: 1) Driving faster than is consistent with the flow of traffic, road surface, atmospheric conditions, visibility, and so on; 2) pushing toward a goal at a rate inconsistent with the orderly unfoldment of all involved elements.

In both cases tensions build, causing impaired reactions, faulty judgment, poor timing. Hurry is the major cause of highway accidents. Likewise, hurry precipitates many of the troubles along life's highway. In every unfortunate incident charged to bad luck, hurry is suspect.

To eliminate hurry and move ahead in balance, three steps are necessary. First, select a goal—something you want to do, have, or be. Second, commit the *way* unto the

Law of Mind. (See Psalm 37:3–6.) Trust it to direct your way and your *rate* of movement. This insures right timing. Third, relax and appreciate the whole trip. Delight in each element as it unfolds; do not wait until the goal is reached. Joy attunes you to inner guidance. Confident in this, you move ahead in ease and balance.

I Am Prospered by Patience

The unhurried processes of nature's unfoldment reveal the patience of Mind. As seed evolves in perfect order and sequence into plant and bloom, this Divine quality is obvious. There is no forcing or manipulation as growth proceeds at its own rate. The qualities of Mind are the qualities of my mind, for there is no separation. Patience is inherent in me. Inner wisdom guides my growth toward spiritual maturity. I trust it and am at peace with my progress.

Patience infuses all of my thinking. I calmly let Divine Intelligence clarify my creative ideas. These are allowed to flow into form and fruition in their own right seasons. I know no sense of hurry, for Mind is never late. I feel no need to force. God's power carries through. Indicated steps I take with ease and confidence that, regardless of any contrary appearances, all is well.

My realization of Mind's perfect, unhurried action extends to and includes every person in my experience. Free of manipulation, my relationships are healthy. I am prospered in all ways as Divine patience governs my consciousness.

I Express Divine Order

The language of creation speaks of eternal verities with compelling authority. Planets proclaim order. Tides tell of rhythm. Seasons sing of sequence. Unmistakable is the message: These qualities are God-ordained, fundamental, and omnipresent. Order, rhythm, and sequence are inherent in Mind and me. Knowing this, I let them pervade my thoughts, feelings, and actions.

Order governs my thinking. The word "accident" is erased from my consciousness. Belief in delay is dissolved. Subconscious patterns of procrastination, tardiness, and resistance are eradicated. My thoughts are established in coordinated patterns. Thus all my relationships with people, places, and things are in accord at their very roots.

From these roots in consciousness my feelings and actions spring and flow in rhythm and natural, happy sequence. I am with the right people at the right time for their good and mine. I am at the appointed place at the appointed hour. I accomplish each task in its appropriate season. My life expresses God's order, rhythm, and sequence.

CHAPTER 14

JOY

Graduations Unlimited

Every day is graduation day in the University of Life. Innumerable are the degrees offered by this venerable institution, though none are honorary. Everyone is enrolled, and there are no dropouts, no holidays or vacations. Tuition is free for those who catch the "school spirit"; it is high for those who do not, and is paid in the coin of illness, frustration, suffering, and unhappiness.

Each day presents a course of lessons designed to acquaint the student with the inexhaustible resources of good. Each evening a higher degree of understanding is received by the one who graduates; that is, learns and benefits from the lessons and *lets them go*. Those who flunk repeat the course. The honor code is self-enforced because we can cheat only ourselves.

Regardless of claims of disgruntled students, the dean of the university is fair. Each enrollee is provided with access to all the answers through the availability of Infinite Wisdom. Furthermore, each evening the graduate, along with the degree of higher understanding, receives a premium: joy—the joy of growth.

TREATMENTS

Today I Am Happy

I am in authority in my world. I alone decide what I shall think—and what I persistently, consistently think determines what I experience. I can allow my thinking to be influenced from the outside, but in the final analysis the ruling decision as to what stays in my mind and what goes rests with me. I bless this unalterable fact because my realization of it makes me master instead of slave.

Right now I decide between two alternatives. I can choose to be happy today—or I can choose to be unhappy. I choose to be happy. Regardless of the outside influences or appearances, I fill my mind with happy thoughts. I love this friendly, beautiful universe in which I live. I soak up its beauty. The wonder of Life pulsating through me floods my consciousness with delight. I am one with Life and one with God. I am happy *today,* and I joyfully anticipate all the happy and fulfilling experiences that await me.

I Delight in the Law

The action of God's laws in the universe, as order, is glorious to behold. The paths of the planets, the flowering of a seed, the fury of a storm all eloquently speak of laws man did not make and cannot change. Yet the laws of gravity, growth, and release of power obey me implicitly as I first obey them. Truly, through law God gave man potential dominion over the world.

I accept the responsibility that goes with dominion. I

appreciate and respect the Law of Mind that establishes me in authority in my world. As surely as the seasons roll, action follows thought. From the inward man the outer man appears. I choose with wisdom and love the thoughts I entertain, for they shape the inner man. I glory in the immutable action of Law that translates them into experience.

Health, harmony, peace, and prosperity flower for me because I plant their seeds in my heart. Permanence of principle is my security for I delight in the law of God.

* * *

The Key to Freedom

Dr. Viktor E. Frankl, the great and wise psychiatrist, discovered the key to freedom while he was an inmate in a Nazi concentration camp. This key unlocked the door of his physical prison and released him into a fulfilling experience of life. He has been sharing this discovery to the benefit of thousands of people ever since. The key is made of four elements that anyone can use, thereby moving from bondage to freedom.

1. *Acceptance of conditions that cannot be changed by outer action.* Early in his imprisonment Dr. Frankl recognized the futility of resisting the inhuman treatment. His mental and physical acceptance conserved his energy. The result was that his mind and body retained a remarkable degree of health. He states that the difference between the attitude of nonresistance and that of mere resignation is life or death.

2. *Freedom to think.* After a few months of bitterly resenting his fate, Dr. Frankl realized that he could choose his own thoughts. No matter what his captors did or said, they could not force ideas into his head. From then on, regardless of circumstances and suffering, he filled his mind with images of beauty, love, and service. He planned ways of communicating his growing understanding of how man's inner world relates to his outer world. Then disciplining himself to exercise his freedom to think, he discovered that he could live above the otherwise intolerable conditions—even the pain of freezing, bleeding feet on forced marches.

3. *Belief in a Higher Power.* While Dr. Frankl never lost his conviction that God is, his concept of *what* God is evolved into the recognition of the Living Presence. His awareness of and reliance on this Presence grew and strengthened. The result was a new vision of life's meaning.

4. *Faith.* An understanding faith develops where principles and power are tried and proved. Dr. Frankl proved the principle of freedom to think. He demonstrated the Power of God within man. As a result, an unshakable faith developed, a faith that rings today in his message of man's inherent freedom.

Wherever you are, whatever your circumstances—the key to freedom is yours.

TREATMENTS

I Am Free

In the unity of God, there is no bondage. I am a free spirit in God's universe, and I declare my freedom from all ties that have held me from my true Self-expression. I *am* the Light of the world. I let this light of truth flood every nook and cranny of my consciousness, and the shadows of error, doubt, and fear evaporate into their own nothingness. I *am* Divine Love. Joyously I let this Love dissolve all resentment, criticism, and self-pity, and the fetters of negativity fall away.

What a relief to be rid of those burdens! I now move ahead easily. Light of heart and confident of step, I delight in each new adventure on the path of my true Self-unfoldment. I allow nothing to violate the integrity of my own soul. The light shines before me, illuminating the way. Love powers my every thought and carries me on to new victories. God rejoices in the free and radiant expression of Spirit which I am.

My Divine Inheritance Includes Freedom

God is the one designing Intelligence and creating Power in the universe. In the perpetual action of creation, the Infinite is forever bringing forth the new out of Itself, including me. In and of the spiritual essence I am formed. By the one Intelligence I am designed. With divine gifts I am endowed.

It is inconceivable that I could ever believe in bondage, weakness, or sorrow; that I could ever consider discord, inharmony, or decay as my lot in life. No place, no condition, no person can hold me in bondage—unless *I* accept that bondage. The wellsprings of life and love are mine on which to draw. The inexhaustible sources of wisdom and power are mine to use. Peace and beauty are mine to feel. Joy is mine to know. "Truly the Lord hath dealt bountifully with me."

Made in the image of the infinite Giver, I give of what I am. Every element of my divine inheritance increases as it flows into expression. Love and peace radiate through my thoughts; wisdom and beauty through my words; life and power through my actions. My joy and freedom of choice sing a blessing and a benediction to all.

*   *   *

The Prospering Power

One desire we all have is the desire to know that we will always have an income ample for our needs. We are not happy with a life of lack and limitation. We want to be prosperous; we *should* be prosperous. In fact, we *are* prosperous—but may not know it.

From Life we have the gift of Creative Power along with the gifts of intelligence to guide it, laws through which to use it, and love to lift it up. This heritage is not something that will come to us by and by as recompense for "all we have been through"; it is ours *now*. We do not have to acquire it; we have to awaken to it. And we awaken to it only as we use it. Muscles are developed by actual exercise, not by *thinking* about exercise. So it is with our Creative Power. The more we use it, the greater becomes our knowledge of it and our trust in it; and the greater our knowledge and trust, the more we will express it in terms of expansive, joyful living.

How do we get started on this ascending spiral? There

is only one way, and that is to decide "I will use my inner Power starting *now*." Not "I'll try," but "I will." No one else can make that decision for us. We must do it ourselves of our own choice, and that very act will start us on the way. Life loves a person of decision, and it is amazing how Life cooperates when our minds are made up.

Thereafter it is a matter of increasing conviction that power is channeled in the direction of our thoughts and feelings; the clearer the thought and the stronger the feeling, the greater the power. It flows through us as we let more energy, enthusiasm, and expectancy flow into everything we do. We are exhilarated by this increase of power. Life looks brighter because we have begun to enjoy it. Prosperity? It follows as a natural result of our prosperous thought and feeling. We could not keep it away if we locked the doors and barred the windows.

TREATMENTS

The Prospering Power Prospers Me

God, the Infinite Giver, is forever giving through all creation. The prospering power of Life is continually prospering Its expressions. As a seed is multiplied by the vital activity within it, so are my creative ideas carried to fruition by the power of life within them. God in me as me is always giving through me. My expanding awareness of this truth assures prosperity in all my affairs.

The illusion of good coming to me from outside myself is permanently dispelled. I look not to fortune, chance, or a hoped-for change in externals to bring me fulfillment.

I look to God, the *one* prospering action, moving in my consciousness as intuition, guidance, love, and creative power.

My crystal-clear perception of wholeness pulses with vitality, and my health blooms. I abide in the fundamental harmony of Life, and my relationships reward me with rich understanding. I know Mind as the unlimited source of money, and my financial activities thrive. Creative power flowing through my God-centered consciousness prospers whatsoever I do.

Divine Mind Guides Me to Abundance and Success

Quietly I contemplate God's omnipresence. I recognize this Presence as God in me, as Life in me. All nature is the abundant proof of the givingness of this Life. It gives abundantly to me as I provide a channel through which it can flow into expression. This channel must be something I can *do,* somehow I can *give,* someway I can *serve.* Divine Mind in me knows which activity will give me the greatest opportunity for true Self-expression and at the same time fill, copiously, all my needs.

Divine Mind is guiding me now in the Right Activity. *It* is opening the way. *It* is sparking the action. *It* is alerting my conscious mind to the necessary outer steps. My success is assured because it is *now* a reality in Mind. It is already beginning to unfold in my life as an experience. Patiently, I watch this timely unfoldment. Eagerly and joyfully I do, give, and serve, with the certain knowledge that I am moving toward rich fulfillment.

CONCLUSION

Thank you, my friend, for joining me in a mental and spiritual adventure—one that has only just begun for both of us. It reminds me of a trail in Colorado that leads up into the high country. It winds through a forest of silvery aspen and blue spruce, past flower-carpeted meadows, and along a roaring stream. Then it climbs up sharply past giant rock formations, molded and twisted by the incredible heat and pressure that formed the mountains eons ago. It reaches over the shoulder of a ridge, around a bend, and *there*—a lake of incomparable beauty, pure sapphire sparkling in the crystal clear air. Mountain peaks tower majestically on every side, and the cool shade of an alpine fir offers an irresistible invitation to rest and to blend with the grandeur and peace.

No matter how many times I have taken this trail, walking along it again is always a fresh new experience. It is an added pleasure when a friend joins me. What joy and excitement there is as my friend discovers something I had missed—that I had failed to see somehow: a rare flower, a gnarled tree etched against the skyline, a quiet pool where the tumbling stream pauses in its pell-mell rush to the valley below.

You, my friend, have traveled with me along a pathway of the mind, and I appreciate your companionship. As with traveling the trail in the mountains, each time you move along this pathway it becomes more familiar. Yet each time it is fresh, as new inspirations unfold to your inner vision. The way becomes personal to *you*. The seven steps are *your* steps as you take them in your own way in your own time. Let the pleasure in discovering new vistas have full sway. And when you discover ones I have missed, I know that somehow, someway, through the avenues of Mind, my pleasure will be enhanced.